Project Management for Parents

Endorsements

Hilary was my project director when she became a parent. As an outstanding employee and a devoted mother, she managed special projects for The Ritz-Carlton, a $6 billion company. Her passion and dedication to her job and family are inspiring. I remember saying to her "I don't know how you do it." Now you can find all of her secrets in this book, and how she uses project management to create excellence at work and organize life at home.

— **Hervé Humler**, Chairman Emeritus and Founding Partner, The Ritz-Carlton Hotel Company

Hilary Kinney has nailed it! Her book should be mandatory reading for anyone who has or is planning to have children. I have been married for 54 years and have three children. Where was a book like this when I was facing the daunting challenge of raising my children in a high-risk environment? Sadly, I had to learn how to achieve a "successful" family unit the hard way—trial and error. I eventually got to implementing most of Hilary's suggestions, but not before having to recover from numerous "errors".

Hilary's book provides an articulate description of the suggested approach and the supporting actions that will increase the probability of achieving a strong family "team". As a successful project manager for five decades, I am ashamed to admit that I never thought of applying proven project management techniques to my "raising a family" project. The insights provided in this book will save parents immeasurable time as they strive to nurture their children.

— **Lee R. Lambert**, Project Management Institute (PMI) Fellow, a Founder of the Project Management Professional (PMP) Certification Program® and Vice President Knowledge Transfer, Roeder Consulting

Hilary is one of the best project managers I have ever worked with, and she has a true passion for quality and leading successful projects. Hilary was instrumental in establishing the Program Management Office at The Ritz-Carlton. Hilary's breadth of knowledge has made her successful in leading multiple types of projects as well as developing new tools and processes. Whether in the workplace or "real life", Hilary makes project management come alive as well as practically apply to many of life's challenges.

— **Len Wolin**, Corporate Vice President, Global Hotel Operations, Club Quarters Hotels

PROJECT MANAGEMENT

MANAGEMENT

for Parents

Engage the **FAMILY**
Build **TEAMWORK**
Succeed **TOGETHER**

HILARY KINNEY, PMP

NEW YORK

LONDON • NASHVILLE • MELBOURNE • VANCOUVER

PROJECT MANAGEMENT *for Parents*

Engage the Family, Build Teamwork, Succeed Together

Published in New York, New York, by Morgan James Publishing. Morgan James is a trademark of Morgan James, LLC. www.MorganJamesPublishing.com

Proudly distributed by Ingram Publisher Services.

Morgan James BOGO™

A **FREE** ebook edition is available for you or a friend with the purchase of this print book.

CLEARLY SIGN YOUR NAME ABOVE

Instructions to claim your free ebook edition:
1. Visit MorganJamesBOGO.com
2. Sign your name CLEARLY in the space above
3. Complete the form and submit a photo of this entire page
4. You or your friend can download the ebook to your preferred device

ISBN 9781631956331 paperback
ISBN 9781631956348 ebook
Library of Congress Control Number: 2021908844

Cover and Interior Design by:
Chris Treccani
www.3dogcreative.net

Morgan James is a proud partner of Habitat for Humanity Peninsula and Greater Williamsburg. Partners in building since 2006.

Get involved today! Visit MorganJamesPublishing.com/giving-back

*To all the parents, stepparents, guardians,
and caregivers doing the best we can.*

We are enough for our kids.

Table of Contents

Preface

The idea for this book came to me during the global coronavirus pandemic in 2020. With schools, offices, and childcare centers closed, parents became teachers and full-time caregivers while still being expected to do their regular jobs. Families struggled, and many became overwhelmed by the workload.

As a project manager familiar with process improvement, I realized that many of the concepts I apply at work can also be valuable at home. Business concepts from project and change management can help us analyze our family lives to make them run more smoothly, whether during a crisis like a pandemic or just the normal rhythm of our daily lives.

I've spent most of my career in project management for a global Fortune 500 company. I've worked on projects ranging from technology and system rollouts to product and service launches, event management, and labor efficiency initiatives. These projects were extremely complicated, encompassing hundreds of tasks, costing millions of dollars, and affecting some 7,000 different business units globally.

I started working in project management in 2003 and have been a certified project management professional (PMP) since 2007. I love project management and the theories behind why we do the work that we do. I am fascinated by all the different parts of various systems and how they all fit together to create successful teams that accomplish big things.

In my personal life, my biggest project was the beginning of my parenting story: adoption. It was a lengthy, emotional project with extensive legal and administrative requirements. My husband and I began the process in the United States with lots of interviews, paperwork, and inspections. There was so much documentation to complete that at one point I joked it was like getting a graduate degree. However, after a year, nothing had happened; we were still no closer to being matched with a child. We then submitted an application to Ethiopia, which has a different set of legal and administrative requirements. However, that country later stopped approving international adoptions, and so we applied for adoption in Uganda. This required a third set of paperwork. Fortunately, my project management experience enabled me to keep track of the long lists of tasks and deadlines.

At this point, our adoption project had been underway for three years in three different countries, but we felt like we were spinning our wheels. It was a disappointing Christmas that year because we had expected to be parents by then. However, little did we know that a miracle was happening at that very moment!

We received a call on New Year's Day that there might be a child for us in the United States. A baby boy had been born on Christmas Day! One month later, my husband and I met our beautiful son! It was an amazing moment; after three years of waiting, we had finally become adoptive parents.

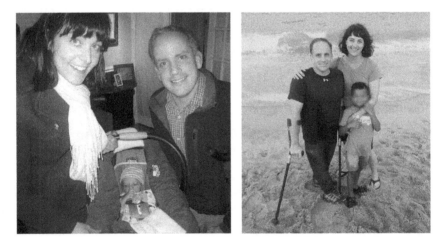

I became a mother later in life, and because I had always greatly enjoyed my career, I wanted to continue working when I became a parent. However, I also wanted to be available for my son and have time to focus on being a mother. I had to take a look at our priorities and capabilities, our family landscape. As the mother of a very active boy, my involvement level needed to be pretty high. I was also assisting my aging mother, along with managing her and my family's medical issues. In project management we acknowledge the constraints of every project—something we'll discuss in more detail later—which proved a good lesson in my personal life. I could not do it all and had to reprioritize my time.

Fortunately, I was able to adjust my work schedule based on my family's needs and my various responsibilities. My project management training helped me to juggle motherhood while continuing to work in corporate project management. The resource allocation and task management methods I used at work, as well as techniques for building high-performing teams and managing change, became increasingly relevant at home. I ultimately found my own balance between my career and motherhood, but we certainly faced challenges along the way. I remember working late at night and on vacations and taking business trips when I really needed to be at home. I sometimes felt stretched in many directions, like there was not enough of me to go around. It wasn't perfect, but we made it happen, to the benefit of both my family and my career. We recalibrated as needed using various project management techniques to support our family journey. And when the coronavirus pandemic hit, we reevaluated our family priorities and made changes to best fit our family and work journeys.

During the pandemic, I started writing on LinkedIn about how project management could help parents, and I found that it resonated with people. The initial article, "Project Management for Parents," was republished on the *IIL Blog* and recognized with a 2020 Most Valuable Post Award.[1] At the International Project Management Day 2020 Conference, I spoke about how the principles of project management could support parents during the coronavirus pandemic. Viewers told me that my speech was enlightening and inspiring and that it helped them balance work and family demands. They also said they wished they had learned these life skills earlier. Sharing that knowledge is at the heart of this book.

My hope is that you'll apply these powerful principles to create a positive and productive environment at home so you can focus on the priorities that are most important, reduce stress, and get more done, while at the same time improving communication and having fun together as a family.

Introduction

As a parent, you can use project management principles to prioritize your family's schedule, improve communication, and streamline life at home, and I'm here to show you how. You'll learn three steps toward building teamwork, getting organized, and succeeding together as a family. Imagine having a professional project manager run your personal life! That's what this book is about: applying proven project management principles to home life so that things work more smoothly.

The beauty of project management is that the same principles can be applied to different types of projects, from building a nuclear reactor to rolling out a new consumer product to managing your child's homework. For example, I'll show you how to create action item lists—which project managers use to track tasks, deadlines, and team-member assignments—to help you better organize your family chores. This book will teach you enough about project management workflow to use these principles at home for multiple types of projects. You can reuse this framework for many different types of projects, which means that developing these skills is a solid time investment.

No matter your circumstances, this book will teach you to analyze your family's needs and develop the best plan to meet them. Throughout the book, I explain the many parallels between parenting and project management using twenty-five real-life examples. Each chapter includes exercises that walk you through how you can apply these concepts to your family. You'll find documents throughout the book that you'll be able to reference as you rethink how to get things done. These templates are a simplified version of the tools that professional project managers use and can apply to a variety of projects at home, from selecting a childcare provider to planning a vacation or moving the family to a new city.

Even though I love the theory behind project management, my goal isn't to come up with more processes just for the sake of doing so. No one has time for busywork, especially parents. Instead, my goal for this book is to provide practical project management advice you can apply to your home life without overcomplicating things or creating unnecessary work. We'll cover many useful techniques in this book; however, you don't have to use them all for every project. Depending on the size and complexity of your project at home, you can select which processes will provide value and be worth the effort. In fact, with any size project, I advise using the least amount of documentation to stay organized. I recommend specific tools for family projects from small to large in Chapter 11 and give you blank templates for additional projects in Chapter 12.

In the corporate world, project management is task focused, but at home you're focused on relationships. I want this book to help enhance your relationships by creating a positive environment, improving communication, and empowering independence. I'll take you through the three *Project Management for Parents* steps: (1) build teamwork, (2) establish your approach to getting the work done, and (3) empower each other to succeed as a family. Because some projects are more complicated than others, I'll lay out the framework and then explain how you can tailor that framework to your situation using different project management tools.

As you read, take notes and bring your partner into the conversation so that you both understand the benefits of a project management approach. As you work through each chapter, discuss what you're learning. Consider where you can apply these principles. What things do you or the family do repeatedly that have become a source of frustration? What large project do you want to accomplish but don't know where to begin? Use the exercises in each chapter to help you work through these challenges. At the end of the book, you'll have completed your learning journey together and will be ready to move forward as a high-performing team.

Project Management for Parents will help you more clearly see the options you have for managing your family life in a way that works for you. The powerful business frameworks that I share can help build teamwork, improve decision-making, and streamline your workload. You'll learn the skills and techniques that professional project managers apply to million-dollar business initiatives, and you'll be empowered to use them to improve your family's life.

Step 1

BUILD TEAMWORK

Chapter 1
Building Teamwork:
Creating Intentional Family Culture

TOP TIPS TO BUILD A FAMILY TEAM:

1. Create an intentional family culture by defining your mission and values.

2. Build teamwork with family activities.

3. Encourage communication and ownership with regular family meetings.

At home, we care for each other and want to enjoy our time together. We have things we need to do, things we should do, things we want to do; in fact, as parents, it seems like we always have too much to do!

The goal of this book is to help families reduce stress by working together to streamline life at home. You'll learn how to apply techniques normally used for million-dollar business projects to manage family life. However, this book isn't meant to turn your house into a super-efficient Fortune 500 company. Rather, I will teach you three steps that will enable you to do more of what matters most: spend quality time with each other. These steps include:

- Step 1: Build Teamwork
- Step 2: Establish Your Approach
- Step 3: Succeed as a Family

The ultimate goal is to foster a loving, productive environment for your family members with shared objectives, trust, commitment, and accountability.

Building teamwork is the crucial first step for a united and positive family work environment. The goal of the second step, establishing your project management approach, is to ensure that everyone is involved and aware of what is expected of them. The last step is to tailor those techniques and empower the family to achieve the results that you want, whether in the area of family dynamics, work, or school performance.

Good teamwork provides a solid foundation for you to succeed as a family, so that's where I'll begin this book. Teamwork means working together to get good results while having fun at the same time, because all work and no play makes for a dull family. At the office, employers use team building to create high-performing teams. We can do the same with our families and have fun while doing it! In this chapter, we'll talk about creating a family culture, building your team, and holding regular family meetings.

Consider a new couple who both have kids from previous relationships. All the people in this blended family have different backgrounds, experiences, and expectations for what a family should be like. How will they know what's expected of them or how to behave if they don't talk about it? That's what active team building is about: sharing experiences, trying to understand each other, and working toward an agreed-upon set of norms for the benefit of each individual and the family as a whole.

Creating a Family Culture

When I talk about defining a family culture, I'm referring to the environment in which your family functions, the tone of the household, and how people interact with each other. Parents can intentionally create the type of culture they want for their family by discussing, documenting, and emphasizing their family mission and core values. This will allow everyone to reach for the same goal and know how to get there together.

I was very fortunate to work for the President and COO of The Ritz-Carlton Hotel Company as Director of Special Projects. The company had an amazing work culture that benefitted both the employees and the organization as a whole. It's remarkable how much easier it is to get work done in an environment where people are equipped, empowered, and encouraged to trust each other. We had fun doing excellent work and achieved phenomenal results.

The reason this culture worked was because it created purpose for the employees. The values of The Ritz-Carlton resonated with the human need for honesty, respect, relationships, and independence. Employees identified with the goal of serving others, including guests and fellow employees, with excellence. People bought into the positive environment and wanted to perpetuate it.

The motto of The Ritz-Carlton is "We are Ladies and Gentlemen Serving Ladies and Gentlemen." This encapsulated the company's values of trust, honesty, respect, integrity, and commitment. They further defined expectations with twelve "service values" that outlined expectations for employee behavior, which included working together as a team.

The Ritz-Carlton's management team asked for employees' input on the culture and documented the values of the organization. They printed those values, which every employee was expected to know, on wallet-sized cards and reinforced them through daily meetings across the organization. These practices sustained the culture over time, which helped the company provide excellent service to guests and win many industry awards.

Families function in much the same way. You'll be more successful with a positive working environment that has purpose. Plus, children will better understand what is expected of them and be more equipped to meet the goal.

What type of culture do you want to establish for your family?

What is your family's overarching goal, and how will you achieve it? Discuss these things as a family and write them down. That way, everyone can remember them and hold each other accountable. Here's how to do that.

Family Charter

To build a strong team, everyone needs to know what the goal is and how to get there. For families, this can be defined with a family charter that includes a mission statement and supporting values. The mission is the overarching goal—what you're striving to achieve. The core values include principles to help everyone achieve that goal. A family charter can be as simple as a list of single words or as complex as a full-fledged essay. I will walk you through how to create a family charter and share some examples later in this chapter.

Charters are especially helpful for blended, adoptive, or coparenting families because they help ensure everyone understands what is expected of them and feels like a member of the team. To create your family mission and core values, first collect the input of the family, then narrow down the ideas, and finally, create your document.

The first step is to hold a family brainstorming session and discuss the type of home environment you want to have. Set aside a scheduled time for this and encourage everyone to share their ideas. Remember that developing your family charter may be an ongoing process that requires more than one conversation. Family charters can also change over time as the children grow and everyone develops different perspectives.

Getting Input and Narrowing It Down

There are a variety of activities that can help initiate a discussion about your family charter—a movie night, art projects, or guided discussions based on the age of the children.

One way to get the conversation started is to watch a teamwork-themed movie. Have a fun movie night, and then talk about what values made this team successful. Here are some questions that may help:

- What was your favorite scene in the movie?
- How did the characters in the movie treat each other?
- What helped them succeed?
- What did they do when they encountered a problem?

For younger children, a creative and hands-on art project can get them involved. Print out a list of values, and let the kids choose their favorites, then glue them on a family picture or cut-out family tree. Another option is to make a collage; take a stack of old magazines and have the kids cut out pictures of what they want their family to be like. Older kids and young adults could use Pinterest to contribute ideas. Have each family member explain what they chose, and then decide together which pieces to include in the family collage.

For elementary school children, here are some questions to facilitate a discussion about how to create a positive family environment and resolve conflict:

- How do you want to feel at home with our family? What are the specific feelings?
- How can we treat each other so that we feel that way?
- How will we act if we have a disagreement?

For teenagers and young adults, here are some questions that can prompt a deeper discussion about the family's mission and core values:

- What do we love to do?
- What words best describe our family?
- What values do we want our family to be based on?
- What helps us do our best? What challenges make it tough to do our best?
- How should we treat each other?
- How should we behave when we have a fight?
- How do we best communicate?
- What does each of us want to be like in the future?

Pick one of these activities that suits your family and that your kids will enjoy. If your children are a range of ages, you may need to vary the activities—for example, have younger children make a collage and have a deeper discussion with the older kids.

Now that you've gotten the family's input, narrow down what you want to include in the final charter. Ask each family member to list words that they want to use to describe your family. You can have each person write the words on sticky notes and put them on the wall or have one person list each suggestion on a large sheet of paper or chalkboard. Then ask each person to explain what they suggested. To narrow down the number of words, have each family member vote by adding a checkmark next to their three favorite words, then add up the results. This enables a quieter person to have input, even if they don't feel comfortable speaking up. The important thing is that everyone feels like they have been heard.

Creating Your Family's Charter

Once you've narrowed down what to include in your family charter, there are several different ways to write it out. A charter can be as simple as a list of words or a statement that represents your mission and core values. Alternatively, you could write several paragraphs. Do what works for your family. If you want to write a mission statement or just list your core values at this point, that's fine too.

For your mission statement, start with a broad, overarching goal of what you want your family to strive for together. This can be a list of descriptive words, a short phrase, or a paragraph. Here are three sample mission statements:

1. *We're loving, servant-hearted, and adventurous.*
2. *We strive to love and serve others and to seek out adventure.*
3. *We'll act lovingly to our family and others. We'll explore the world through travel and outdoor adventures. We'll serve others and our community.*

Your core values are a more detailed list of principles that support your mission statement. Again, this can also be a list of single descriptive words, short statements, or a series of paragraphs with specific actions. Here are three examples:

1. *Brave, encouraging, forgiving, generous, honest, kind, and responsible.*
2. *Honor each other, explore new places, steward our resources, and support our local community.*
3. *We'll create an environment of love and fun at home with family dinners, movie nights, games, and lots of hugs. We'll live a healthy lifestyle providing what our bodies and minds need through wise choices.*

    We'll go on vacation together at least once a year, go camping twice a year, and spend time doing outdoor activities together on weekends. We'll explore new parts of the world when possible and learn about other countries.

    We'll treat each other with respect by honoring our differences and calmly voicing our opinions. When there's a conflict, we'll address the issue quickly in a straightforward and respectful manner.

    We'll be responsible with our resources and belongings. We'll strive to do our best at work and at school by being diligent and using our natural talents. We'll support our community in promoting the wellbeing of children and hunger relief.

As you're working through this, give the family time to think through and process it. Post the draft in a common area so family members can see it, think about it, and add feedback and ideas. It can be a discussion topic over meals to see if there are new insights. Don't worry about it being perfect; you can update it later. Try one version for a few weeks, and if you want to change it, you can. It is more important to capture the family input and have it to refer to going forward.

Once you've chosen the final words to describe your family, write them down to preserve them. Display it in the house, and I'm sure the kids will be happy to remind others about the principles and hold them accountable! You can simply post it on a sheet of paper on your fridge, or you can have it laminated or framed and hang it on a wall.

To keep the conversation going, you can use current events to discuss examples of healthy and unhealthy values. For example, if there was a robbery in your community, you could talk about how it compares to your family values. To reinforce the positive environment, acknowledge your kids when they model the family charter. Creating and maintaining a positive family environment is worth the effort and will be foundational to the success of future projects as well.

Team-Building Activities

Now that you've set the mission and core values for your family, let's talk about how to keep the positive environment alive through team building. The goal of team building is to learn how to work together through shared experiences so that people better understand each other and feel connected as a group. The family accomplishes these shared experiences in an enjoyable way, which lays the groundwork for successfully completing other projects together, like chores. Team-building activities can also be useful in staying connected with your kids as they get older.

Team building can be accomplished through icebreakers and indoor and outdoor activities. Icebreakers are games in which you share insights about each other, activities you can do during meals or other family times. Indoor and outdoor activities take a little more planning, but these shared experiences create family memories that can last a lifetime. Try to do at least one team-building activity a month with your family. Here's a list of ideas:

Icebreakers

- **Would you rather?** Give people a choice about what they would rather do. For example, would you rather run like a cheetah or fly like a bird? Would you rather be good at coloring or dancing? Would you rather live your life with no phone or no video games? Eat burgers or nuggets? Vacation at the beach or in the mountains? Ride a bike or skateboard?
- **Two truths and a lie.** Have each person think of two truths and a lie about themselves. Then share the three statements and have the others guess which are the truths and which is a lie. If a person guesses correctly, they get a point. The person who earns the most points wins.
- **Penny for your thoughts.** Collect pennies or other coins that were minted in different years. Have each person pick up a coin and share something memorable that happened in the year printed on it.
- **Question of the day.** Ask a question to better support one another: What's your biggest pet peeve? What gets you out of a funk? What do you need when you get upset/sad/angry?
- **Jokes.** Have each family member share a silly joke.
- **Inspirational quote.** Have one family member share a quote and then discuss what it means.

Indoor Activities

- **Movie night**. Have regular movie nights and let the kids pick what you watch.
- **Talent show.** Share talents (dancing, singing, etc.) individually or in teams.
- **Game night.** Have a game night with board games or puzzles or use one of the ideas below.
  a. Blind drawing: One person describes to another what to draw but doesn't say what the object is. Then the rest of the family tries to guess what the drawing is.
  b. Birthday line-up: Have the family line up in order of their birthdays without talking. If someone speaks, you have to start over.
- **"Make Your Own Meal" night.** Have a pizza night during which everyone builds their own pizza, makes their own burger, or decorates their own cupcake. After the meal, have a race to see how quickly everyone

can clean up the kitchen together. Keep track of your clean-up time and see if you can beat it the next meal!

Outdoor Activities

- **Scavenger hunts.** Go on a scavenger hunt; you can divide into different teams or work as a group. Provide clues that lead sequentially to the final prize. This can also be done indoors.
- **New skills.** Learn a new skill together like meditation, painting, kayaking, archery, etc., or take on a team-building challenge like a ropes course.
- **Sports and activities.** Participate in activities together like hiking, skiing, fishing, etc.
- **Field trips.** Go on a field trip to visit a museum, a nearby town, a farm, or a monument, or have a picnic in a park.
- **Service project.** Participate in a community service project like cleaning up litter in a park or in your neighborhood.

As parents, it is important that you're aligned and communicating with each other as leaders of the family. One way to do this is regularly spending time together through your own team-building activities. Make time for each other and go for walks, have a coffee, or go on a date night at least once a month. By deliberately building teamwork among all of your family members, you'll create a more positive environment and learn to work together while having fun at the same time.

Family Meetings

Family meetings are another way to build teamwork and parallel project status meetings. During these meetings, discuss how things are going and get everyone's input to create a collaborative, effective working team. Regular family meetings ensure everyone is communicating and has their say. They provide a safe place for people to express frustrations before they boil over and to work together to solve problems before they become unmanageable.

In corporate project management, each team has regularly scheduled meetings. These meetings serve as venues for progress updates, working sessions, and problem-solving time. I also use these meetings for team building and usually start with an icebreaker. These exercises not only teach the team more about each other, but also how to be more understanding and work better together.

During one project I managed, I encountered a team that was very reserved and quiet. My goal was to lighten up the work environment, build teamwork, and make team members laugh. So I opened each meeting with some of my son's favorite knock-knock jokes. At first, the team didn't know what to think; they were afraid to laugh, and it was awkward. Then they started to loosen up, and the most reserved team member cracked a smile. When they started to volunteer their own jokes, I knew I had achieved my goal! Seeing this reserved group evolve into a collaborative and fun work team felt like a big accomplishment.

Family meetings can be designed around what works for your family at the time. Perhaps you have some reserved teenagers and the environment could use a little lightening up, or maybe you have little ones with short attention spans. You can design these meetings to be ten minutes or less by doing a quick check-in with all family members to see how things are going. The foundation of the meeting is to find out what worked well and what challenges the family faced this week and decide what the goals are for the next week. Ask simple questions. You can use the analogy of a rose, which may be easier for younger children to understand. The fully bloomed rose represents something beautiful and positive; the thorn represents something uncomfortable and negative; and the flower bud represents the promise of the future, a flower that's about to bloom. Below are the three questions Bruce Feiler popularized in his book *The Secrets of Happy Families*.² I've added the rose analogy here to show you how you could use these questions with younger children:

1. What worked well this week? Where did we have a fully bloomed rose?
2. What did not work well this week? Where did we find thorns?
3. What will we work on next week? Where do we see flower buds?

The key here is to get kids involved and encourage them to provide input. Celebrate the positive and refer back to the family charter. Come prepared with examples, like how a child represented the family value of honesty by admitting to breaking a glass. If something comes up that isn't working well—perhaps mornings before school are too rushed—talk through possible solutions. Get everyone's input on how to make things go more smoothly and decide what you want to try the coming week. You could decide to make lunch and select clothes the night before. Then set goals to meet them; for example, the kids need to be dressed by 8:00 a.m. You can also ask the kids what they think their reward and punishment should be for meeting or not meeting the goal in the next week. Perhaps if they are dressed by 8:00 a.m. every weekday, they'll earn a trip to the ice cream store on Friday.

These meetings will take some humility and understanding from all family members, but especially from parents who have a more authoritarian perspective. Receiving negative feedback can be difficult, but it's essential to ensure you're building and improving the family culture and function. Think of it as a great opportunity for everyone to learn and grow, as it empowers kids and parents to think creatively and take ownership over the family function.

For example, in one of our family meetings we discussed how we were frustrated by my son's complaining about his writing homework. So we all decided that my son's goal for the next week was less complaining when asked to do writing. Our son came up with the reward of ten minutes extra screen time for meeting the goal and a punishment of five minutes less screen time if he missed the goal. He understood what the consequences were, thought they were fair since we agreed to them, and was motivated to meet them.

By having input on the family function, your kids will feel empowered and have ownership over (and therefore buy-in for) the work. Kids can evaluate their own work, building their critical thinking and problem-solving skills. The family meeting is also a useful way to stay engaged with teenagers and keep communication channels open.

Saturday morning or Sunday evening can be good times to have the family meeting to set the expectations for the week ahead. You can also add a team-building activity into the family meeting, like telling jokes or playing a game. Do what works for your family; remember, the format can vary each week.

Example: Building Family Teamwork

A newly blended family recently moved in together, and the kids are having a lot of conflicts and misunderstandings. One family previously had a very quiet household with no loud arguments or yelling. The other side of the family is very boisterous and opinionated and enjoys heated debates over the dinner table. The couple decide to take a proactive approach to building teamwork within their new family.

One night at dinner, the parents have them play a game of "Two Truths and a Lie." Each kid shares three statements, and the rest of the family guesses which are true and which is the lie. The next week they play the game "Penny for Your Thoughts." They hand out pennies with different years, and each person shares something memorable that happened that year. The third week they hold a talent show and share many laughs. Both families learn new things about the other members, and they start having fun together. The couple continues to hold these weekly events to build camaraderie.

Once the kids get to know each other better, the parents decide to create their blended family charter. They start with a movie night watching *The Incredibles* and talk afterwards about ways the family in the film worked together well and where they struggled to work as a team. The next week the parents ask the kids to complete the following three sentences.

1. As a family we want to feel...
2. To create those feelings, we'll...
3. When there's a disagreement, we'll...

This is what the kids came up with.

1. As a family we want to feel love, respect, and laughter.
2. To create those feelings, we'll spend time together, create blended traditions, and seek understanding of our individual differences and different pasts.
3. When there's a disagreement, we'll be honest and respectful to resolve the conflict in a timely fashion while giving each other space as needed.

The following week, the parents ask the kids to help create their family mission statement by providing three words that they want to describe their blended family. Then the family decides as a group which words to use in the mission statement. They settle on "Our Family is Accepting, Understanding, and Fun." Then the parents have their new blended-family charter framed and display it in the dining room. The house is a lot more peaceful, and when they do have conflict, they refer to the values to remind them of what they agreed to.

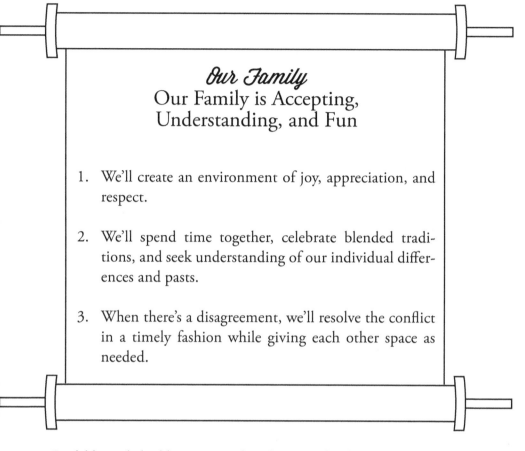

Our Family
Our Family is Accepting,
Understanding, and Fun

1. We'll create an environment of joy, appreciation, and respect.

2. We'll spend time together, celebrate blended traditions, and seek understanding of our individual differences and pasts.

3. When there's a disagreement, we'll resolve the conflict in a timely fashion while giving each other space as needed.

By deliberately building teamwork within your family, you create a community, set a bar for everyone to meet, and clarify expectations in a positive way. Even when you encounter problems, you know that the team has been built to support each other and work through them. Teamwork binds the family together and creates a firm foundation for successful future projects.

Exercises

Exercise #1: Create Your Mission and Core Values

Have a family discussion about your mission and how you'll bring that mission to life through your core values. Then document your mission and put it on display where everyone can see it: framed and hung on a wall or laminated and posted on your fridge. Here are several different options to create it.

A. Have a team-themed movie night and then discuss what the characters did to work together. Here are a few movie ideas: *Cool Runnings, Finding Nemo, Ghostbusters*, any of the Harry Potter movies, *Lilo & Stitch, Lord of the Rings: Fellowship of the Ring, The Sound of Music, The Incredibles, The Mighty Ducks, Toy Story*. Here are some suggestions for conversation starters:
   a. What was your favorite scene in the movie?
   b. How did the characters in the movie treat each other?
   c. What helped them succeed?
   d. What did they do when they encountered a problem?
B. Make a family values tree. Print a list of values for family members to reference (see suggestions at the end of the chapter). Each member selects the values that they want included and explains why. The values can be cut out or written on leaves and glued on a paper tree. The mission statement could be represented as the roots or written above the tree. Another option is to frame a family picture and write the mission and values on the mat surrounding the picture.
C. Collect magazines you no longer want and let the kids cut out examples of words and images that represent what they want the family to be like. As a group, discuss what they selected and how you can create that as a family. Then make a family collage with the different pictures and hang it up it for all to see.
D. Have a discussion with younger children about the mission and core values by using the following questions:
   a. How do you want to feel at home with our family? What are the specific feelings?
   b. How can we treat each other so that we feel that way?
   c. How will we act if we have a disagreement?

E. For older children, have a deeper discussion about the mission and core values by using the following questions:

    a. What words best describe our family?

    b. What do we love to do (activities, hobbies)?

    c. What values or character qualities are important to us?

    d. How do we bring these values to life?

    e. What helps us do our best? What challenges make it tough to do our best?

    f. How should we treat each other?

    g. How do we communicate best?

    h. How should we behave when we have a fight?

    i. What does each of us want to be like in the future?

    j. What difference do we want to make in the world?

    k. What goals do we have?

Exercise #2: Schedule an indoor or outdoor family team-building activity on the calendar.

Exercise #3: Select a day for the weekly family meeting. Ask the following questions during the meeting:

- What worked well this week? Where did we have a fully bloomed rose?
- What did not work well this week? Where did we find thorns?
- What will we work on next week? Where do we see flower buds?

Here is a reference list of values to generate ideas.

Accepting	Generous	Loving
Adventurous	Gentle	Patient
Calm	Gracious	Peaceful
Comforting	Grateful	Polite
Committed	Hardworking	Respectful
Creative	Healthy	Responsible
Disciplined	Honest	Self-controlled
Educated	Honoring	Service oriented
Empowering	Hopeful	Thorough
Encouraging	Humorous	Transparent
Faithful	Integrity	Trustworthy

- Forgiving
- Fun
- Joyful
- Kind
- Understanding
- Wise

Chapter 2
Creating Family Champions: Encouraging Ownership

TOP TIPS FOR CREATING FAMILY CHAMPIONS:

1. Ensure parents and other project leaders agree on the reasons for and benefits of the project.

2. Communicate project benefits and status early and often with your "team."

3. Support the family members emotionally and functionally through the project.

W e all want harmony at home, with family members working together toward the same goal. Wouldn't it be great if our partners and kids enthusiastically responded to working on a project—like champions of the cause? The project and change management techniques I'll cover in this chapter can support that transformation. Project management can be used for small to large endeavors: from improving communication and organizing chores to applying to college and moving the family to a new town.

Because projects come in many shapes and sizes, having a supportive team makes all the difference. To get projects done, you need people to do them, and you also need processes to manage the work. In short, project management is made up of people and processes. The first section of this book covers the people side of projects, and the second section covers the processes.

> *Project Management = People + Processes*

People are the most important part of any project. High-performing teams emphasize ownership, engagement, and communication. Ensuring support of the project, helping participants understand the benefits, and communicating throughout the project increase the chance of success. Implementing these methods is the first step toward creating family champions.

First let's talk about the different groups of people involved in a project. These are the people who need to be included in order to create family champions who are working together for the same goal. Picture a triangle with a small group of leaders at the top: the parents. The project working team—the family as a whole—is in the next section. The support team is at the bottom of the triangle; these are the people who support the family, like caregivers, but aren't a part of the family. These people will be impacted by family projects but aren't working on them directly. The people involved may vary by project, as could their level of impact. For now, we'll talk generally about how the strategies of ownership, engagement, and communication start at the top and flow down to everyone else.

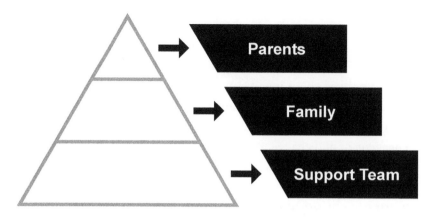

Ownership

Leaders provide the resources (money and authority) to make the project happen. "Ownership" means that the leaders of the family support the project. In families, leaders are the parents, guardians, or stepparents, depending on the situation.

This was a difficult lesson for me to learn as a project manager. I would wonder why a project wasn't going anywhere, and more often than not, the reason was simple: there was no support for the project from upper management. It may have been a great idea, but the organization had other priorities at the time. I learned that if this was the case, there was no use in spinning my wheels; I ought to move on to projects that were a priority for leaders in the organization.

The same is true at home; it's vitally important for you and your partner (if you have one) to both be enthusiastic about a project and agree on what you're trying to achieve. Otherwise, the project simply won't be successful.

Before you invest a lot of time or energy in a family project, talk with your partner to gauge their level of interest. Conduct research to gather all the necessary information. This process will inform the project leaders/parents so they can decide whether there's enough interest to move forward. One person operating in a vacuum will not be able to make something happen. If your partner isn't supportive, the project should be shelved or revisited later.

An example from my family illustrates the importance of being aligned on an important project. The idea of pursuing adoption started with me. At first, I sat on the idea for a while, prayed about it, and thought about how to share this *big* idea with my husband. It's not like I could go ahead with an adoption plan without my husband's support. During premarital counseling, we both said we were about 50 percent interested in having kids; it was not a big priority for either one of us, but it was not off the table either. That conversation had occurred five years earlier. We hadn't revisited it since then, so I wasn't sure what he would think now. We talked about it and eventually agreed that adoption was the right choice for us. But first we had to explore what it meant to us and what could be the impact, risks, and benefits in order to fully understand the decision. That's where engagement and change management—the people side of change—come in. We'll explore those concepts next.

Engagement—Supporting the People Side of Change

People need to be involved and see the benefits of doing something before they will support it. The concept of change management can help get them there. Change management is a business discipline dedicated to supporting the people implementing the changes required by a project. It addresses both the functional changes people need to adopt and the emotional impacts of whatever changes are being implemented. Below I'll explain how involving people in project planning, communicating the project's benefits clearly, and supporting them through the process helps ensure long-term success.

To encourage people to become champions of a project, you need to get their input from the beginning. The more involved people are in the planning process, the more engaged and cooperative they're likely to be. No one wants to be told what to do when they haven't been consulted first. Change management helps ensure that people support the project, which will make it easier to implement and more likely to succeed.

It's useful to think about the size of a project and its impact on various members of your family. How much will the project affect them on a personal level? If a project will impact them financially or physically, like a job change or move, they'll have a stronger reaction to the changes and will require more support to make the transition. They may respond with sadness or anger, become resistant, and refuse to do the work. Bigger change means a bigger response; smaller change means a smaller response.

What challenges are people facing in other areas that might affect their ability or willingness to accept the changes required by the project? If there are a lot of other changes going on in their lives, they may find it more difficult and take longer to make additional changes. Thinking in advance about people's capacity for change will help you predict how they will respond to new projects so you can be prepared to support them through the transition.

For example, if a parent accepts a new job that requires the family to move, this is obviously a big change that will receive some pushback. To help your family accept their new reality, involve them early in the process so they aren't taken by surprise. There are functional tasks that must be completed, like finding a new home and packing up the furniture, but you also want to ensure the people impacted, like your spouse and kids, are emotionally supportive of the move.

The emotional change response is similar to the grief response: denial, anger, bargaining, depression, and acceptance. For example, if you're moving to a new town, your children may first deny that the move is happening. Then they may get angry and dispute whether you should move, bargain to stay at their current school, and feel depressed for a while before they can accept what's happening. By experiencing all these emotions, the family better prepares themselves for the transition. It wouldn't be a good idea to tell your children about the move late in the process and just say they need to be happy about it! By allowing them to participate, both intellectually and emotionally, in the change from the beginning, you'll help them feel better prepared and respected as active participants.

ADKAR Model[3]

The Prosci change management process identifies how people can successfully adapt to change by using the ADKAR model (Awareness, Desire, Knowledge, Ability, Reinforcement). ADKAR was created by Jeffrey Hiatt, the founder of Prosci—a global change management research and training company used by many Fortune 100 companies. By supporting family members to reach each of these five outcomes, you'll make them more apt to adopt the changes.

- **Awareness** of the need for change.
- **Desire** to support and participate in the change.
- **Knowledge** of how to change.
- **Ability** to implement required skills and behaviors to make the change.
- **Reinforcement** to sustain the change.[4]

Let's use the example of teaching your child how to ride her bike. Does she understand that riding a bike is an essential skill and will give her something fun to do with her friends? Then she has accomplished the first step: awareness. Is something stopping her from making the effort? If so, you can use the AD-

KAR Model to help assess where she is stuck. Did she fall off her bike and hurt herself, and now she's scared to try again (desire)? Does she want to learn but hasn't received enough instruction (knowledge)? Is she just too young (ability)? Or has she not had enough practice to remember and bolster what she's learned (reinforcement)?

I was surprised by how long it took my son to learn to ride his bike. He had strong desire and even asked to have his training wheels taken off before he was ready, which meant we had to put them back on again. He saw the older kids without training wheels and wanted to do the same but lacked the ability. It just took time for him to develop enough coordination and balance. Now, after a lot of hard work and moving through all the stages identified by the ADKAR Model, he loves to mountain bike and jump off ramps and curbs!

What's in it for Me?

The principle of "What's in it for Me" (WIFM) is another valuable part of change management. In other words, why are you doing this project? What are the benefits? Think it through with your partner to make sure the project makes sense. Are the benefits worth the time, cost, and risks? Make a pros and cons list. The benefits of moving to a new town could be a higher income, career advancement, or closer proximity to relatives. The negatives might be leaving your friends behind and managing a major life transition. Is this move still something you want to go through with? If so, create a list of reasons so that you can communicate them to the family.

Communicating the reason behind each project is important; the family will understand why they are doing it and can buy in. If the family is moving to a new town for a parent's promotion because the household income will be higher, it's important for everyone in the family to know the benefits in order to give them purpose. The family move will have a higher likelihood of success when they support it.

Next, think of a short pitch, sometimes called an "elevator speech," about why you're moving so that you can share it with people who are important to you. For example, you could say something like "We're moving because I got a new job, and we'll be closer to Grandma and Grandpa. We'll be sad to leave friends and change schools but excited to try something new." Identify the emotions and articulate the reason for the move to your kids and others impacted so that they can better understand this life transition and start moving through the emotional part of the change.

Parents foster the family's desire to make change by creating awareness and understanding of the need for the change. Those first two steps in the ADKAR Model—awareness and desire—lay the foundation for the long-term support of the project.

Communication

Once the parents have agreed to the project, know why they are doing it, and can share the benefits, it's time to think about communicating all of these things to other people who will be affected. Think back to the triangle of groups of people at the beginning of the chapter: parents, family, and support teams. Now is the time to identify the different groups impacted by the project and how best to support them through communication.

Identifying Your Project and Support Teams

Let's identify the different groups of people working on the project. The project team consists of those working directly on the project, like family members. Support teams are affected in some way by the project but don't work on it directly, like caregivers, relatives, teachers, coaches, church leaders, community organizations, housekeepers, coworkers, doctors, etc. These people help your family be successful, so it's important to identify them and include them in communications. Since the project team is more immediately affected, you'll want to communicate with them early and often. Support teams require fewer and less frequent communications.

> *Who's on your family' support team?*

You can use the templates at the end of the chapter to brainstorm lists of project team members and support teams. Give yourself some time to think of everyone impacted, as the support team list will probably grow throughout a project. Other family members can also add to the list.

For a family move, the leaders would be the parents, the project team would be the kids, and the support teams would be relatives, friends, neighbors, school administrators, coworkers, movers, and realtors.

Once you've identified your support team, keep their contact information in a central place. Include names, titles, email addresses, phone numbers, mailing addresses, etc., on the list. I usually keep a contact list in an Excel tab on my computer so it's all in one place and easy to reference. Here is an example of a contact list.

Name	Title	Company	Phone Number	Email
Jolene Doe	Client Services	A1 Moving Co.	101-232-4567	jolenedoe@a1moving

Establishing Your Communication Plan

Now that you've identified your project and support teams, it's time to develop your communications plan. The higher up on the triangle someone is, the more frequently they should be consulted. When developing a communications plan, consider (1) what should be communicated to make sure everyone is clear on expectations; (2) what types of communication would work best, such as in-person conversations, phone calls, texts, emails, and/or letters; (3) how often those communications should happen.

Communication plans can be used for large or small projects or just family life in general. If a blended or divorced family wants to improve communications, this template can serve as a roadmap to help you talk through and identify needs. A benefit of using this template is that it takes some of the emotion out of the discussion and allows you to identify people's tasks objectively. A newly divorced family could talk, in a structured way, about how and when they want to communicate regarding after-school activities and homework.

For a large project such as a family move, it's useful to keep this information on one document so you can remember it, track it, and mark it when completed. The project team (i.e., the family that is moving) may be talking about updates every day at breakfast or dinner; in other words, communication may be primarily verbal. Support team communications may be less frequent but more formal: emails sent to school or realtors, cards sent to neighbors, phone calls made to relatives. It's also useful to identify who will be responsible for each communication, which allows you to distribute the work and clarify responsibilities. For example, the kids could communicate the move to their teachers and friends, and the parents could communicate to school administrators.

Here's a sample communications plan. I've included a template at the end of this chapter so you can make your own.

Communications Plan, Family Move Project					
To Whom	*What*	*When*	*How*	*By Whom*	*Status*
Kids	Status of move	Daily	Dinnertime	Parents	Ongoing
Aunt Janice	Inform of move	Feb. 1st	Phone Call	Dad	Done
Moving Company	Inform of move date	Feb. 15th	Email	Mom	Done
Schoolteach-er	Inform of move	Feb. 15th	Verbal	Kids	Planned
School Ad-ministrator	Inform and re-quest school records	Feb. 28th	Email	Dad	Planned

Once the communications plan is created, it should be actively used and regularly monitored. To keep all family members engaged, you'll need to continuously communicate about the project and its benefits. Involve them early and keep them informed throughout the project. This frequent communication will keep your champions engaged, answer any questions, and allow for faster problem-solving.

Stalemates

What should you do if your spouse or family doesn't want to participate in a project? For example, what if you've accepted a job in a new town, but some members of your family aren't on board? Consider these steps.

- Look at your value proposition and WIFM list. Do you have a clear picture of the benefits and risks, and have these been clearly communicated to your partner and family? If not, communicate in a way that they may more easily understand, such as discussing it while on a walk, writing them a letter, or asking them if they have any questions.
- Ask whether you've involved your family in the planning process enough for them to be comfortable with the change. To help them feel included, let them help choose your new neighborhood or home, pick out a new paint color for their bedroom, etc. Tell them about the area you're moving to and explore it online, look at pictures, and find activities they enjoy.

- Think about where a reluctant family member is in the stages identified by the ADKAR Model and where they might require more support to facilitate the change. Do they know at some level that the change is needed but still don't want to make it happen? Transparency is important, so be honest about the positives and negatives of the change you're planning. That kind of transparency can be useful to help them see that the change is important, while at the same time acknowledging that it won't be easy. Give them time to process their emotions and go through the grieving process. Don't be surprised at their anger, negotiation, or depression; talk with them about those feelings.

- Support them during the move. Host a going-away party with their friends, work together to pack up their room, or facilitate them meeting new friends by setting up playdates with neighbors or signing them up for local activities. Let them know their preferences are important by allowing them to pick out new bedroom furniture or a restaurant in the new town to visit when you arrive. Continue to check in with them after the move to see how they are doing and provide additional emotional and functional support, as necessary.

Using these ownership, engagement, and communication techniques can improve teamwork at home. By involving family members and creating awareness and support, you can get buy-in up front and encourage them to accept and adopt the change.

Example: Changing Schools

The parents decide together that a new school is the best choice for their child. They research the schools and determine that the advantages outweigh the disadvantages. The parents come up with a list of benefits and rationale for why this change is necessary. They talk first with the child who is changing schools, share the reasons, and give them time to start going through the grieving process. They think through how to support their child with this change, like sharing information about the new school and going to visit it. Then they generate a list of all the people impacted by this change—current school, future school, friends, teachers, etc.—and write out their communications plan. As they move through this change, the parents allow their child time to mourn leaving their old school and to talk through their feelings. The parents support their child through the change by hosting a going-away party with their old friends and scheduling get-togethers once they have changed schools. These steps provide the emotional and functional support to equip their child for a smooth school transition.

Projects that are supported by family champions are constructive and successful. Using the techniques of ownership, engagement, and communication allows these projects to be done more smoothly and positively.

Exercises

Exercise #1: Support Team List

List all the people who impact your family function, regardless of any one specific project. Then rate their level of impact on family life on a scale of 1–5, with 1 being low and 5 being high. This will be your family's "support team" list, which you can reference for future projects, when the list may be smaller.

Here is a list of people to consider: caregivers (babysitters, nannies, daycare providers), grandparents, relatives, teachers, coaches, church leaders, community organizations, housekeepers, coworkers, doctors, landscapers.

Support Team	Level of Impact (1 [low]–5 [high])	Notes

Exercise #2: Communications Plan

Fill in this communications plan template for your project.

Here is a list of potential projects to help you generate ideas: communications plan for a blended or divorced family, coaching a sports season, planning a school event, or a family move.

Communications Plan, Project _____					
Who	What	When	How	By Whom	Status

Step 2

ESTABLISH YOUR APPROACH

Chapter 3
SEEING THE STOP SIGN:
A REALISTIC FAMILY PLAN

TOP TIPS TO ESTABLISH A REALISTIC FAMILY PLAN:

• •

1. Understand and recognize the constraints impacting your family.

2. Rank your family's priorities and determine if there's a neglected priority.

3. Use these constraints as a personal decision-making framework.

• •

N ow that you know how to build teamwork for a united and supportive family work environment, it's time to establish your project management approach. In this step, you'll identify your priorities and apply project management techniques in order to achieve them. These techniques also ensure that everyone is involved and aware of what is expected of them to streamline life at home.

Family life is busy, and managing our family schedules can seem like an insurmountable challenge. It can feel as if we're pulled in too many directions, without enough time to rest and relax. Sometimes we just want to say, "Stop the madness!" This is where the power of project management can help, by helping us clearly see our options and prioritize them to achieve the life that we want.

I find it useful to look at family life in the context of constraints used in project management. A constraint is any limiting factor or restriction, like time or money. There's only so much time or money available for any project.

A constraint is a limiting factor that affects the execution of a project.[5]

–PMBOK Guide

Though constraints may seem restrictive, they keep your family from overreaching by providing guardrails to protect your most important priorities. Focusing on constraints is the opposite of what many of us often do: cram as much into our schedules as possible. We work full-time, the kids are in three or four different activities every week, and we spend hours commuting every day. Maxing out our schedules may work for a short time, but it takes a huge toll on our family quality of life. In this chapter, I'll explain how project managers use the concept of constraints to help with planning, and I'll show you how you can use it to clearly think through your family priorities. And in the next chapter, I'll show you how to rearrange your priorities to achieve the life you want.

The three classic types of constraints in project management are time, cost, and scope.

- Time is the duration it will take to complete the project.
- Cost is the financial price of the project.
- Scope is the amount of work and the quality level of the end product.

Typically we represent three constraints or limitations using a triangle, sometimes called the "iron triangle" because these are hard limits that can't be exceeded. Project management uses these as a framework for evaluating competing demands and adjusting if necessary.

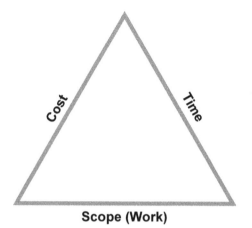

Scope (Work)

Cost, time, and scope are interrelated and impact each other. The greater the scope, or work, that needs to be done, the more time and money will be needed to complete it. If the amount of required work decreases, then the time and cost go down as well. For example, building a two-story building costs less and takes less time than building a four-story building.

Another way of thinking about it is a triangle-shaped water balloon. The water in the balloon represents the amount of work, time, and money required, and the balloon itself represents the limits of cost, time, and scope. If one part of the project gets bigger (like the amount of work), the water must move from the other parts of the balloon to support it. Because the balloon can only stretch so far, it limits the overall amount of work that can be accomplished. If you try to increase the work too much, the balloon bursts.

In a work project, the project manager takes care of the water balloon and makes sure it doesn't pop. Project managers continually adjust for scope, time, and cost to keep the project manageable. One of my favorite questions to ask at the beginning of a project is, "What is the number one priority?" This tells me how to run the project to make sure that priority is met. If meeting the budget is the first priority, I make sure not to let project changes cause a budget overrun. If quality is the first priority, I may extend the deadline to allow more time to focus on the work. We move the water around from one tip of the triangle to the others to support the most important priority. This framework for decision-making requires a balancing act, and the same can be done in our families.

For example, when we had our kitchen renovated, the most important constraint was time. We had to get the renovation completed by Thanksgiving, when we were hosting family. The countertop was the last piece of the renovation to be completed, and it was especially important because you can't start cooking a meal without one. The countertops arrived two days before Thanksgiving, and I noticed a small ding in the surface. However, since family was arriving in a few days for dinner, I decided to accept the dinged countertop so that I could start cooking. In this case, the quality of the countertop was less important than the time constraint.

Family life is complicated by multiple demands. In this chapter, we're going to talk about our families' constraints and what we are and aren't capable of accomplishing. What are our hard limits? How can we keep our balloons from bursting? Let's take a realistic look at everything that must get done and how it all fits together so that we can achieve the family life we want and need.

Family Constraints

Constraints are interrelated restrictions that can't be exceeded. These constraints impact each other, and if one changes, it will affect the others. Parents must balance constraints in the way that best benefits everyone in the family. Since family life is more complex than a work project, I've identified some additional constraints that impact families. Family life has at least eight constraints:

1. Time
2. Budget
3. Kids' Education
4. Parents' Work
5. Family-related work
6. Extracurricular activities and hobbies
7. Health and safety
8. Quality of life

> ### *Constraints are limitations that cannot be exceeded.*

Let's break each of these down:

Time, something none of us have enough of, is an inflexible constraint that doesn't change.

Budget, which includes the financial resources you have as a family, also tends to be a relatively inflexible constraint that's difficult to change. When we discuss this constraint, we will generally be referring to your earnings from work and not savings or investments.

The remaining constraints are more flexible and easier to make changes to. These include:

Parents' work, which relates to the parents' jobs or careers. That may include full-time employment, part-time employment, side gigs, etc.

Children's education, which includes your kids' entire school career, whether that's homeschooling, public school, or private school. This also includes college or graduate school if that's a goal for your family.

Family-related work, which includes everything that has to happen to keep the family running, such as housecleaning, grocery shopping, laundry, and taking the kids to doctors' appointments.

Extracurricular activities and hobbies, which apply to both parents and kids. For parents, these could be volunteering, going to the gym, attending church, or a book club. Kids could be involved in after-school sports, clubs, competitions, or activities.

Health and safety, which encompasses anything that affects the overall physical or emotional health of the family. This could include, for example, regular sleep and exercise or pre-existing medical conditions that take time to manage, such as kids with special needs.

Quality of life, which represents family time and satisfaction—things that improve your family life in some way. This could mean rest and relaxation, vacation, or spending time with relatives or friends. In my family, it means outdoor activities, games, and dinners together. Although quality of life often seems to end up at the bottom of our priority list, it is extremely important for our long-term health and family relationships. I would venture that most of us would like a higher quality of life and more time together.

You can think of these constraints in relation to a child growing up. For example, consider how constraints on the parents are affected by the child's age. As a baby, the biggest constraint on the parents is time because the baby requires 24/7 supervision and cannot take care of himself. When he becomes a toddler, the biggest constraint is safety, because he's learning to walk and requires protection to stay safe. When he is in elementary school, education is the highest constraint because he's learning how to be a student and developing the foundation of his education. When he enters middle and high school, activities and health and safety become constraints as he learns to be more independent. When he enters college, the family budget becomes a big constraint (if the parents are paying for it). The point is that as your family changes, your family plan may change as well.

I found I was often caught off-guard by family-related work; for some reason, this constraint didn't really make it on my radar screen! I frequently wouldn't allow enough time to get chores done. Before becoming a parent, I would spend most of my hours and energy on work at a high-stress job, going in early and getting home late. After I became a parent, I realized my approach had to change, because I would be exhausted from work and not have enough time in the evenings or weekends to get the laundry and cleaning done—let alone anything just for me, like exercise or a hobby.

The eight constraints listed above represent the different components of family life and will be unique for each household. They all fit together to create each family's lifestyle and require making trade-offs—in my case, a slightly messy home in exchange for more time at work. I find it useful to consider each of these areas holistically and see how they impact family life overall.

The Stop Sign

One way to illustrate these eight constraints is a stop sign. The sign reminds us that we should not exceed any of the eight constraints or we may be crossing a line into a dangerous situation. As parents, we can look at our constraints and decide how best to address them given our unique situation. By identifying constraints, we can more easily determine our priorities and what works for our family.

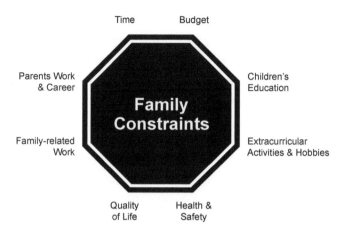

The Family Plan in the Middle of the Stop Sign

Let's consider how a family plan fits within these constraints. Think of your family plan as a circle in the middle of the stop sign. The family circle is filled with a limited amount of time, money, requirements for school and career, family-related work, extracurricular activities, quality of life, and health and safety.

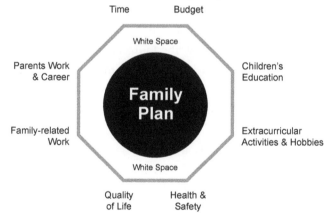

If you want, you can fit your family plan into the constraints such that the circle bumps up against the sides of the stop sign. In other words, your life is maxed out. Alternatively, you can plan for a smaller circle that allows some breathing room. For example, if a family decides to schedule a lot of extracurricular activities and two full-time jobs, their circle will be bigger. If they decide that only one parent will work full-time and the kids will have fewer activities, their family circle will be smaller.

A related consideration is how much "white space," or unscheduled time, you want in your family plan. White space is extra time that isn't blocked out or scheduled. My mother-in-law once said to me that she wished we had more white space in our lives so that we could relax more and not be so busy. I think that's very wise advice—to intentionally create downtime in your schedule so you can have more free time.

Families run into problems when one of their constraints exceeds the boundaries of the stop sign. There's only so much time in the day or money in the bank. If a family consistently goes over budget, that could lead to bankruptcy. If parents don't have enough quality time together, that could lead to marital issues. If long hours are required at the office, that could lead to physical illness or the kids feeling neglected. Let's consciously look at family constraints and make decisions to get to the family plan that we want.

What are your family priorities?

Establishing your priorities as a family informs the rest of your decisions. You'll know what's first in line and what other constraints should come after it. You can make the rest of the family plan work when you know what comes first.

For example, for a young family, the budget may be the biggest constraint because they may not have much income or savings. As a result, their careers would be another major priority because they support the budget. Other items like activities and hobbies may fall lower in the list of priorities because they cost money.

For an older family whose kids are about to enter the workforce, quality of life may be the highest priority. The family may want to make lots of memories together before the kids leave the home. Therefore, they may spend more of their budget on activities together or vacations to enhance their time together.

When I became a parent, I read that we have 940 Saturdays with our children before they turn 18. It was a good reminder for me, especially since my father died unexpectedly when I was a teenager and I wished that I had more time with him. I wanted to make the most of the time that I have with my son and had to take a realistic look at our family priorities. My child and my family's medical issues both took up a lot of my time, plus I needed to work. I've learned that my body can only put up with so much stress before something goes haywire. I had a two-page medical resumé of ailments, including seven surgeries, and I didn't want to add to that list. How could I balance everything? The project management principle of constraints showed me that I couldn't do it all and had to reprioritize my time. I decided to pull back on my career when my son was young because I couldn't mentally, physically, or spiritually handle a full-time corporate job while being a new parent. I'm not superwoman. We reevaluated our family priorities and made changes to best fit our situation.

Take time to think about what your family priorities are and what you want them to be. Step back and see if one area has become too high of a priority or if another area is being neglected.

Example: The Effect of the Coronavirus Pandemic on Family Constraints

As an illustration, let's talk about what happened to working parents during the coronavirus pandemic. Typically, before the pandemic, we would go to work, the kids would go to school, and then they may have gone to after-school activities. Eventually, we would all come home and (hopefully) spend at least part of the evening together. In other words, before the pandemic, most families' top priorities were the parents' work and the kids' education, and these constraints were fairly clearly defined.

So what happened when the pandemic hit? Health and safety became a top priority. Schools and childcare centers closed, people were spending more time at home, and parents became teachers and after-school daycare providers. Basically, parents' workload at home tripled. Parents took on all of that extra work because school didn't provide as much support and childcare was limited. That means their family plans greatly exceeded the stop sign of constraints. This would be like your boss tripling your workload without providing additional resources, causing the theoretical project balloon to burst.

This was an untenable situation for most families, and we saw the effects. Forty percent of working parents quit or reduced their hours due to the pressures of managing online work and school during the COVID-19 pandemic, according to research by career website Flex Jobs.[6] Approximately 865,000 women dropped out of the labor force when the 2020 school year started based on data from the United States Bureau of Labor Statistics.[7] These effects illustrate how families had to adjust their plans by prioritizing health and safety and reducing the constraint of parents' careers to meet the kids' necessity for education and supervision. These families had to take a hard look at their constraints and make some difficult decisions about changes to their family plan.

During the coronavirus pandemic, I also made the decision to scale back my work schedule to assist my son with online school. Fortunately, my husband was employed full-time and took on several side jobs to provide for the family. Our top constraints became our family's health and safety and my son's education, and our family budget was reduced as a result. We reduced extracurricular activities and home services to accommodate the decrease in budget. In other words, we rebalanced our family plan based on the changing constraints of the time.

Considering this stop-sign framework can determine what success looks like for your family. Every family is different, and looking at these constraints can provide a window on your family landscape and allow you to evaluate what is realistic. You can see how these constraints are interrelated and use this as a decision-making framework.

In the next chapter, we'll look at how we can analyze and change a family plan using the stop-sign method in more detail. This stop-sign framework can be used at different times as your family situation changes.

Exercises

Exercise #1: Family Priorities

Rank the constraints in descending order of priority for your family, with one being the highest and seven being the lowest. Then rate your level of satisfaction in each area from low to high. Although time is an important constraint, since it is inflexible, it isn't included in this exercise.

Constraint	Current Ranking (#1-7)	Satisfaction Level (low, med., high)
Budget		
Kids' Education		
Parents' Work/Career		
Family-related Work		
Extracurricular Activities		
Health and Safety		
Quality of Life		

Chapter 4
Running the Stop Sign: How to Reprioritize the Family Plan

TOP TIPS FOR WHEN YOU HAVE RUN THROUGH THE STOP SIGN OF CONSTRAINTS:

• •

1. Evaluate family constraints in current and preferred level of impact.

2. Make desired changes by adding resources or deprioritizing workload or environment.

3. Identify items that are in and out of your new family plan.

• •

I s your family plan too ambitious? Are you constantly stressed out? Do you feel like there isn't enough of you to go around? Have you run through the stop sign of constraints and don't know how to slow down? Wouldn't it be nice to know when we have exceeded our limitations and have a warning system for when we should stop before something goes wrong?

The good news is that project management can help! Just like parents at home, project managers are constantly juggling to make it all work; budgets are cut, there aren't enough employees to get the work done, and the project must move forward with limited resources. Like project managers, parents can adjust based on their unique situations. The stop sign introduced in the last chapter is a useful method for considering the size of your family plan and whether any changes need to be made.

Using the Stop Sign for Decision-Making

To adjust a family plan that's too ambitious, let's first categorize the eight family constraints to see how we can address them. We'll look at which ones are more or less flexible to see how we can impact them. Bundling these constraints together illustrates their overall impact on the family plan.

> *Constraints can be categorized as more or less flexible.*

More Inflexible Constraints
Resources
1. Time
2. Budget

Although time and budget are important resources, they limit all the other factors, and they can't be adjusted as easily. As a result, time and budget are categorized as more inflexible constraints.

More Flexible Constraints
Workload / Scope
1. Parents' work and career
2. Kids' education   *Environment*
3. Family-related work   1. Quality of life
4. Extracurricular activities and hobbies. 2. Health and safety

The other constraints are more flexible and can be divided into two areas: workload and environment. Workload includes four constraints: parents' careers, kids' education, family-related work, and extracurricular activities. Environment includes quality of life and health and safety.

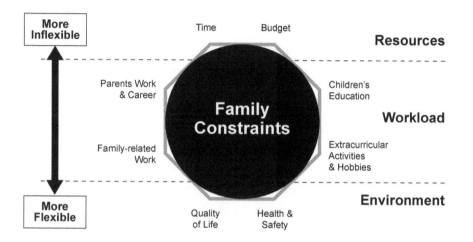

These three categories of resources, workload, and environment can be changed to rightsize the family plan to fit into the stop sign. This means deciding which constraints will receive higher priority and adjusting the others accordingly. This exercise is like a balancing act that requires moving parts around to find where they fit best.

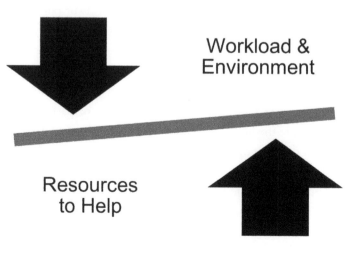

There are three options when trying to shrink the family plan to make it fit within the stop sign of constraints: decrease your workload, place less of a priority on your environment, or increase your resources.

1. Decrease your workload (work inside and outside the home, education, or activities)
   - Decrease parents' work hours
   - Decrease family-related work
   - Decrease kids' educational activities
   - Decrease extracurricular activities and hobbies
2. Deprioritize your environment
   - Focus less on health and safety (but only to a point!)
   - Adjust your expectations for quality of life
3. Increase your resources (time, budget)
   - Use more money to get the work done
   - Hire or include people to outsource the work
   - Extend the timeline, move the work to a later time, or cancel it

Adjusting the More Flexible Constraints

First, let's look at how the more flexible constraints of workload and environment can be decreased to rightsize the family plan. The general idea is to reduce the amount of work or add resources (people or services) to do the work. Here are some options to make the family plan fit inside the constraints.

To decrease your overall workload: Is there work either at your job, at school, or around the house that can be reduced? Can the kids or parents cut back on activities? Or can you outsource some of the work to take it off your plate?

- Are there ways that the parents' work schedules can be adjusted to accommodate other constraints? For example, could one parent work early in the morning or late in the evening so they can be home with their kids during the day? Could one parent transition to part-time work or not work outside the home at all to support other areas of the family plan?
- Consider different options for your children's education, like public school, private school, or homeschooling. Also, consider your expectations for your children's academic performance. If you expect them to get straight As at a private school, this will be more time-consuming and expensive.
- Family-related work, like chores and housecleaning, can be addressed in several different ways. If your budget allows, you can hire house clean-

ers or a meal delivery service to reduce your overall workload. If those things are unaffordable, can you bring in other resources like relatives to watch the kids or have the kids do more chores around the house? Or do you just let certain things slide for a while because you know your family has other priorities right now?

- Extracurricular activities and hobbies are probably the easiest area to cut back. Maybe your kids could reduce the number of activities they're involved in for a certain amount of time when the family has other priorities and then resume those activities later. In addition, parents could spend less time volunteering or engaging in social activities to prioritize other areas of the family plan.

Next, let's consider your family environment.

- Quality of life: This is important but often gets pushed to the side. I would be cautious about deprioritizing this area too much, as it is vital for your family's long-term wellbeing. However, you might want to consider whether there are areas that you can intentionally focus on so you can scale back in other areas. For example, perhaps reduce family dinners to fewer nights per week or cut back somewhat on family recreational time; make the time you do have together count by staying totally focused on each other (instead of, for example, sitting in the same room while everyone is on a different electronic device).

- Health and safety: These are necessary, of course, but what that looks like is somewhat different for each family. For example, in my family, this is a high constraint. My son and I have numerous food allergies and intolerances that must be managed closely: gluten, corn, dairy, nitrates, garlic, and xanthan gum. Several of these ingredients are in most gluten-free and prepared foods, so I have to make most of our food from scratch. This takes a large amount of my time, which I factor into our overall family plan. As a result, my family's health and safety remains a high constraint. By contrast, although everyone likes home-cooked meals, perhaps they aren't really necessary for your family. In that case, using prepared meals or ordering take-out periodically would allow you more time for other things.

Adjusting the More Inflexible Constraints

Time and budget are more inflexible, but there are ways to adjust them. For example, although time is static, you can do less or change when things get done. In addition, your budget can be adjusted with effort by reducing expenses and finding new sources of income.

- To create "more time," perhaps you can move or forgo something. Can an activity be pushed back to a later time? Plan for it later in the month or year or cancel it altogether.

- The budget is often difficult to increase, but you can decide what you're spending money on to reduce your costs. Can you reduce expenses to preserve the integrity of your overall budget? Can you increase your budget by picking up a side job?

You'll need to decide which constraints make the most sense for your family to adjust. This can reduce the guilt of comparing your family to other families who may (for example) have their kids in a lot more activities. You know that you have made an intentional choice and have chosen the right balance for your family. Remember that the goal is to shrink the family plan overall so that it fits into the stop sign of constraints. Consider what constraints can change to achieve a workable family plan.

Slowing Down and Stopping at the Stop Sign

As an example, let's think through options for an overwhelmed family with four busy kids and both parents working. We can look at reducing the workload and adjusting resources (time and money) so that their family plan fits within the stop sign of constraints.

Here's an example of what their situation might look like:

1. Time—wish for more time in the day
2. Budget—need to pay for kids' tutoring and activities
3. Kids' education—school plus tutoring
4. Parents' work—Dad and Mom work full-time
5. Family-related work—Mom wants more support with chores around the house
6. Extracurricular activities and hobbies—too many kids' sports and parents' activities
7. Health and safety—need to manage ongoing family medical conditions

8. Quality of life—weekends feel rushed and wish for more quality time together

It seems like this family has a lot going on. But like in our own lives, we may not realize the impact of how all these different components fit together. Let's analyze this family's situation further to better understand their family plan and circle size. We'll look first at their current situation and then at where they would like to be. We'll then add a numeric weight to each constraint and see how those weights add up to the family circle size.

Constraints are ranked on a score of one to four, with one being the lowest weight and four being the highest weight. The constraints that impact the family situation the most have the highest weight.

- 1 = lowest weight
- 2 = moderately low weight
- 3 = moderately high weight
- 4 = highest weight

The total weight shows the size of the current family plan:

- 19–24 = large circle; maxes out everyone's time and energy
- 13–18 = moderate circle; manageable with some white space
- 7–12 = small circle; manageable with more white space
- 0–6 = tiny circle; too much white space and not enough work getting done

Although time and budget are important constraints, they limit all the other factors and can't be adjusted easily (in the case of the budget) or at all (in the case of time). As a result, time and budget are not included in the charts below.

Current Family Circle

FAMILY CONSTRAINT	CURRENT SITUATION	WEIGHT (#1-4)
Parents' Work	Mom and Dad work full-time.	4
Kids' Education	School plus tutoring	3
Family-related work	Big house requires lots of cleaning and maintenance.	4
Activities & Hobbies	Parents volunteer two times per week, and kids have four activities per week.	4

Health & Safety Needs	Ongoing family medical conditions have to be managed.	3
Quality of Life: Rest and Relaxation	Weekends are full of activities and errands, and they feel rushed.	1
Total Weight, Current Family Circle		19

Total Current Family Circle Size = 19/24, large circle; maxed out

You can see that with many categories at the highest weight (a "4"), this family plan is nearly maxed out at a weight of 19 out of a possible 24. Work, school, and activities are taking up essentially all of their family plan and aren't leaving much time for quality of life or family-related work. They are likely stressed and not feeling very close as a family. They should make some changes before something goes wrong. Specifically, they can reduce the focus on certain aspects of their family life to better balance their family plan.

Desired Family Circle

Now let's think about this family's desired situation. We can change their approach to each constraint and corresponding weights and see how it impacts their family plan.

FAMILY CONSTRAINT	DESIRED SITUATION	WEIGHT (#1-4)
Parents' Work	Same	4
Kids' Education	Same school but no tutoring	2
Family-related work	Pay house cleaners and other service providers to do some of the work.	2
Activities & Hobbies	Parents volunteer just one time per month, and kids have just one activity per week.	2
Health & Safety	Same	3
Quality of Life: Rest and Relaxation	Increase family time together and take more vacation time.	3

Total Weight, Desired Family Circle	16

*Total Desired Family Circle Size = 16/24,
moderate circle; manageable*

In this example, the family decreased the number of activities, eliminated tutoring, and hired people to help around the house. The family also added weight to quality of life. With these changes, the size of the family circle still decreased and became manageable at a total of 16 out of 24. They could even add more weight to quality of life and still be in the range of a manageable family plan.

IN and OUT of Family Plan

Now that this family has decided what changes they are going to make to reach their desired family plan, here's an outline of their different focus areas. Writing down what is now "in" the family plan and what is "out" of the family plan, and posting it as a reminder, keeps them accountable to uphold it.

In Family Plan:
- Both parents work full-time
- One extracurricular activity per week for parents and kids
- Housecleaning and landscaping service
- Family dinner three times per week
- One family outing per week
- Two family vacations per year

Out of Family Plan:
- Tutoring
- More than one activity per child per week
- Parents volunteering more than once per month

By consciously identifying your constraints and what is in and out of the family plan, you can find a balance that's fairer to all family members. It's also more likely to stick because you've expressed the changes in detail and explicitly stated the goals.

Example: Short-Term Work Projects

A couple has two school-age kids, and both parents work full-time. The mother is given an important short-term work assignment that requires travel two days a week. At the same time, the father wins a contract with a new client that has a short deadline. They realize that their work will take up a lot of their time for the next two months. The parents look at their constraints to see what they can move around during this period to make it possible to complete these work projects.

First, they ask his retired parents to pick up the kids from after-school activities and spend time with them until the parents get home. Then they schedule a house cleaner and set up grocery delivery, including lots of prepared foods. One of the kids' birthdays is coming up, and they decide to hold it at a kids' play place that provides all the food and decorations instead of having it at home. They also let their church know that they are not available to volunteer during this time. At the end of the two months, they book a weekend away together so they can reconnect as a family and celebrate the end of the work assignments.

In summary, the parents can't reduce the work focus, so they add resources (grandparents and home services) to reduce their workload at home and also decrease volunteering to add more time in their schedule. Then they make sure to reprioritize quality of life by spending time together as a family when the assignments are over.

You can see that by changing the focus on different areas of the stop sign, you can rightsize your family circle for long-term or short-term needs. Every family is different, and looking at these constraints can provide a decision-making framework to help you evaluate what is realistic for your family. Using this stop sign can determine what success looks like for your family.

The exercises below will run you through this framework to determine your current and desired family plan to rightsize it.

Exercises

Exercise #1: Current and Desired Family Plan Comparison

Complete the current and preferred weighting of your family's constraints and see how they add up to your family circle size. There are two charts to complete, one for the current plan and one for the desired plan. This is also a useful exercise to complete when there are big decisions to be made or changes in your family, like an additional child. You can use this exercise as a decision-making framework to see the impact on your family and your desired outcome.

Constraints are weighted with a score of one to four, with one being the lowest weight and four being the highest. The constraints that impact the family situation the most have the highest weight.

- 1 = lowest weight
- 2 = moderately low weight
- 3 = moderately high weight
- 4 = highest weight

Current Family Circle

Consider these different constraints. Which ones impact your situation the most. Which ones have the highest weight? How much weight does each one of these have in your family right now? Use a score of 1–4 to assign numbers to each area.

FAMILY CONSTRAINT	CURRENT SITUATION	WEIGHT (#1–4)
Parents' Work		
Kids' Education		
Family-related work		
Activities & Hobbies		
Health & Safety		
Quality of Life: Rest and Relaxation		
Total Weight, Current Family Circle		

Total Current Family Circle Size = ___ /24 _____

The total weight shows the size of your family circle:

- 19–24 = large circle; maxing out
- 13–18 = moderate circle; manageable with some white space
- 7–12 = small circle; manageable with much white space
- 0–6 = tiny circle; with need for more to be done

Desired Family Circle

Now that you've considered your current situation, think about your desired situation. For example, are your activities impacting your quality time too much? If you spend many hours volunteering or at kids' sports competitions and it's harming your quality of life, it may be time to consider changing the focus areas.

FAMILY CONSTRAINT	DESIRED SITUATION	WEIGHT (#1–4)
Parents' Work		
Kids' Education		
Family-related Work		
Activities & Hobbies		
Health & Safety		
Quality of Life: Rest and Relaxation		
Total Weight, Desired Family Circle		

Total Desired Family Circle Size = ___ */24* _____

The total weight shows the size of the family circle:
- 19–24 = large circle; maxing out
- 13–18 = moderate circle; manageable with some white space
- 7–12 = small circle; manageable with much white space
- 0–6 = tiny circle; with need for more to be done

Exercise #2: IN/OUT of Family Plan

Now that you have adjusted your constraints, write out specifically what has changed to rightsize your family plan. What is IN your family plan, and what is now OUT of your family plan?

In Family Plan:

-
-
-
-

Out of Family Plan:

-
-
-
-

When your IN/OUT Plan is complete, post it in a common area, like on the fridge, to remind you of the new guidelines to achieve the life that you want.

Chapter 5
Getting on the Same Page: Establishing Your Scope

TOP TIPS TO GET ON THE SAME PAGE:

1. Parents/leaders agree on the rationale, design, and budget of each project.

2. Discuss the project scope with other family members and get their input.

3. Share the plan in a kick-off meeting.

With your priorities identified, let's figure out how to move toward your goals. We want everyone on our team to have a basic idea of what's happening and why we are doing the work. We do this by creating a high-level project outline, called a "scope definition." Perhaps one of your new priorities is quality of life, so you want to build a treehouse in the backyard for the kids to play in and to go on a family vacation together. To take this next step, we can outline these projects so everyone can see the plans and ensure that the family is literally "on the same page."

Defining the scope with your family team helps everyone align toward a common goal, understand the work that needs to be done, and stay engaged. As we discussed in Chapter 2, a key component of a successful project is involving the people who are affected to get their input and buy-in. The more involved people are in the planning process at the beginning, the more cooperative they're likely to be. The scoping discussion lets participants voice their opinions and have input on the design, which usually leads to a better result. Another benefit is that, by discussing and summarizing the plan at the beginning, you're better prepared to start the work since you have a roadmap of what needs to be done. A defined project scope also decreases misunderstandings later on.

A scope definition covers the who, what, why, when, and how of the project. This includes the rationale for the project, what is being done or created, the people involved, and the budget. It also can be used to outline project timing, though that's often difficult to determine this early in the project because the scheduling will evolve. The action item list, covered in the next chapter, is the next step and provides more detailed information for each of these components. But for now, we'll create a high-level overview.

Consider a project you want to complete at home and think through it as you read this chapter. To illustrate, I'll use two examples: building a treehouse and planning a vacation. Let's break down the scope of these projects.

Why—The Rationale

The first part of your project scope should explain why you're taking on the project in the first place. What are benefits and the specific measurements that will make it successful? Think about what created the need for this project; why do you want to go on vacation or build a treehouse? Understanding the need for a project is useful because it helps you ensure that the project's design and management deliver the results that you want.

For example, is the main goal of a vacation to relax, learn something, or have an adventure? This was a conversation my husband and I should have had earlier, before he planned our honeymoon. He had planned a very active honeymoon of white-water rafting, horseback riding, and jungle tours. All of these were great, but I also wanted some relaxing time at the beach. Fortunately, we had this conversation before the trip, but it would have saved a lot of work if we had discussed it earlier.

Once you know why you're doing the project, consider how you define success. Outcomes should be measurable; otherwise, how will you know whether you've accomplished what you set out to do? They can be measured in completed tasks or emotional responses. For example, when building a treehouse, your desired outcomes could include finishing it in a reasonable amount of time while ensuring that it's safe and fun for the kids. For a vacation, your desired outcomes could include relaxation and seeing select tourist attractions.

For family projects, get the kids' input on their definition of success. For example, ask them what they want to get out of vacation and incorporate some of their ideas. This will help them feel included and give them a sense of ownership of the project. It could be as simple as going fishing or eating s'mores—anything that will make them feel heard and be more excited about the trip. As a kid, I remember visiting every famous tourist site on busy family vacations, and it was exhausting. I wanted time to relax, not to cram in every educational moment possible. I guess you can see a theme here; I enjoy a little downtime on vacation!

What—The Design and Deliverables

Now that you know why you're doing the project, you can move to designing it. What do you want this project to look like? What are you going to do or create for this project to meet the requirements of the people participating in it? Get the family's input so the project can be designed for everyone. If the project is a treehouse, requirements would include things like the location, number of rooms, number of windows, and paint color. For a vacation, the requirements may be a dinner at a favorite restaurant, a day at the beach, or a kayaking trip. In the next chapter, we'll explain more about how to get the actual work done. For now, let's focus on the overall project design.

Here, again, your kids are important stakeholders and probably have some great ideas, so get their input. Activities to encourage involvement can be creative and playful; for example, have them draw or cut out pictures of what they want the treehouse to look like or what they want to do on vacation. A brainstorming session can be a good place to start. With brainstorming, there are no bad ideas; everyone should be allowed to contribute without being criticized. Have one person write down everyone's ideas for other people to build on, which will help get the creativity flowing.

Also consider what quality level you want to achieve. Will only the very finest treehouse or vacation be acceptable, or are you willing to settle for something less than perfect? These expectations will impact the budget and overall design of the project.

Once you've designed what the trip or treehouse will look like, other important elements include planning tools. For a vacation, this could be a trip itinerary. For a treehouse, this would be a design plan. These more concrete items, called "deliverables," support the overall planning process.

Each project will have a distinct design, and people may have different input and opinions. The parents (leaders) can determine the final design once they have gotten all the input and can weigh it against other parameters, like budget.

Who—The People

Now that you know what is being created, you can determine who should be involved to make it happen. At this point, you already know who the leaders will be—you and your partner. Also consider the rest of the project team. Think about what roles are necessary and then who can fill them. In the case of a family vacation, this would include who is going on vacation, as well as who will be heavily involved in the planning, like a travel agent. Also identify who's indirectly involved in the project. Do you have someone to pick up your mail? Does summer camp know that your kids won't be there for a week? Do you have a house sitter or dog sitter? Creating a list of people who are involved in or impacted by the project ensures you don't forget anyone who's critical to the project's success. The list can always be updated as the project moves forward and more information is available.

When considering who you want to be involved in the project, think about their availability and whether they can participate. Would someone else be better, or should the project be postponed to accommodate someone's schedule? Figuring this out now keeps you from getting stuck later when a key person isn't available. For example, if you want your handy uncle to assist with building the treehouse, find out when a good time for him to do it is so that he's available.

Outlining the decision-making process can reduce misunderstandings as well. Does everyone have to agree, or are you content to get input and then make the final decisions? If several family members are involved in vacation planning, clearly explain up front how decisions are being made so no one is disappointed or feels left out.

How—The Budget

Of all the elements of your project, the budget has the greatest impact and a high potential for conflict. As a result, you'll want to establish an overall budget at the beginning, before the project moves forward, although it may take time to get prices for specific items. The budget is usually decided by the leaders and the amount finalized later once more details are determined.

For example, when we decided to renovate our kitchen, my husband and I had different levels of comfort with the budget, and it was causing conflict! I wanted to spend less money, and he wanted to spend more. Once we agreed to the budget (after a few tense days), it was much easier to make decisions on the kitchen design, and our relationship improved. Determining the overall budget and how to handle the funding at the beginning sets clear expectations for everyone and informs the rest of the project planning.

When—The Timing

Similar to the budget, the timing may be tentative at the beginning. While it's useful to discuss timing in general, you may not be able to confirm it until later. For example, when planning a vacation, you could discuss now how long you want the vacation to be. Note that you may not be able to confirm actual dates until further along in the planning process, once you've got things like hotels and transportation in place.

Blocking out milestones provides references for the overall timeline. For instance, if you'll get the best price by booking airplane tickets six weeks out, then you want to determine the destination eight weeks beforehand. These milestones provide structure and can serve as a reality check on how soon work should begin.

One mistake to avoid is setting deadlines based on incomplete information. As a project manager at work, I often have to persuade executives not to commit to a project due date until more of the details have been confirmed. It's often impossible to determine a final due date early in the process, and waiting until more accurate information is available prevents misunderstandings and delays.

What If—Risks

Now that you've been through the five major components of scope definition, let's consider risks. Risk management involves preparing for things that could affect the project. What are things that could delay or derail your plans? What could happen that would risk completing your timeline, blow your budget, or detract from the experience?

Thinking about this at the early stages helps identify potential challenges so you're prepared to address them. We'll dive into risk management in more detail in a later chapter, but at this point, think about the things you should consider as you move forward with this project. For a tree house, a major risk might be that the tree can't safely bear the weight of the structure. For a vacation, bad weather or illness might be potential risks. You'll need to identify these risks so that you can address them.

Scoping Process

When defining scope, I find that a one-page document is useful to get the conversation started. You can have an initial conversation as the parents or leaders to quickly capture all the different areas of the project: why, what, who, how, when, and what-if. Then involve the family to develop the scope in more detail. There's a template at the end of this chapter to work from.

The scope is the early definition of the project and doesn't have to be perfect. Don't expect to know everything at the beginning, as it will take time to get all the information you need to finalize the scope.

It is also useful to clarify what won't be included in the project to ensure that everyone has clear expectations. For example, if you're planning a family vacation, you can clarify that the vacation only includes immediate family members and not friends or extended family, or that it will last one week and not two. Stating what isn't included may seem like too much detail, but it's beneficial to define the parameters of the project to reduce misunderstandings later.

When you're working through the scope process, it may be enough just to talk about these components with your partner and family. If it's a large project or if project team members live apart, you might want to write it down and keep it on hand for reference. At work, I send the scope document to the project leaders and ask them to confirm their understanding and support. Depending on the level of project complexity and the relationships between people working on the project, you may want to do this as well to document the work and budget and reduce miscommunication.

Once you've decided on the scope, share the final version with the entire family. Tell them the why, what, who, how, when, and what-ifs. You can discuss this exciting new project in a family kickoff meeting. Use this time to set expectations and explain roles and responsibilities. Review the details of the scope document and answer any questions. This could be simply done over a meal or during a family meeting for longer conversations. Doing this work up front will reduce confusion and provide a solid foundation for moving forward with the project.

Example: Event Planning

To plan a surprise wedding anniversary party for grandparents, the family can discuss the why, what, who, how, when, and what-if with other family members. Below is a sample scope document that can be shared with the family for feedback and then used for reference as the project progresses.

SCOPE DOCUMENT	
Project Name: 50th Anniversary Celebration	Date: November
Why/Rationale/Success Metrics (Why are we doing this and what are the benefits?) We are holding a surprise dinner to celebrate Jim and Sandra's 50th wedding anniversary. The event will bring the family together and honor Jim and Sandra's legacy. The event will be low cost so that all family members can participate.	**What-if/Risks** (What are potential risks of doing this?) Risks are schedule conflicts, Jim and Sandra discovering the surprise in advance, and family disagreements.

What/Design & Deliverables	Who/People Involved:
(Brief description of project and requirements)	*Leaders:*
• Restaurant selection within 20 miles of their home	• Stephen and Anita
• Invitations	*Project Team/Roles:*
• Restaurant contract and menu selection	• Dan—create and send out invitations
• Slideshow of pictures and memories	• Nicki—restaurant and menu selection
• Commemorative book of slideshow	• Loretta—getting Jim and Sandra there
• Speeches	• Sam—decorations
• Event Agenda	• Caleb—slideshow
Out-of-scope (to keep costs down):	• Angie—commemorative book
• DJ	• Katie—emcee/agenda
• Flowers	• TBD—speakers
	Invitees (Support Team):
	• Family only: Jim and Sandra, their kids and grandchildren
	• Not included: friends and coworkers
How/Budget	**When/Timing**
(How is this being funded and what is the amount?)	*(List major milestones and expected timing)*
Each family will pay for their meals, plus split the costs of the facility rental and commemorative book.	• Inform family of idea: December/January during holiday get-togethers
	• Confirm family availability: mid February
	• Book Restaurant: late February
	• Send Save-the-Date: early March
	• Send invitations: early April
	• Event: Week of May 5th—their 50th anniversary week!

Putting together a scope document for family events has multiple benefits. Having a scope document supports smooth planning and teamwork by defining the key components and addressing everyone's questions and concerns. Identifying a budget and listing out-of-scope items reduces misunderstanding later. In the case of the anniversary party, for example, that may mean agreeing that the dinner is only for family, not friends or coworkers, which provides a clear explanation for who gets invited. Identifying and communicating goals at the beginning helps everyone voice their needs and aligns the family on a common objective.

In summary, a scope document gets everyone "on the same page" in understanding the key components of a project. It provides an overall picture to use as the project moves forward.

Exercises

Exercise #1: Scope Document

Complete this scope document for your project.

Project Name:		Date:
Why/Rationale/Success Metrics *(Why are we doing this and what are the benefits?)*		**What-if/Risks** *(What are potential risks of doing this?)*
What/Design & Deliverables *(Brief description of project and require-ments)*		**Who/People Involved:** Leaders: Project Team: Support Team:
How/Budget *(How is this being funded and what is the amount?)*		**When/Timing** *(List major milestones and expected timing)*

Chapter 6
DEFINING THE WORK: IDENTIFYING AND DOCUMENTING ACTION ITEMS

TOP TIPS TO IDENTIFY AND DOCUMENT WHAT TO DO:

1. Research tasks from previous projects and get expert input.

2. Be clear and break down each task so it is manageable and age appropriate.

3. Use the simplest documentation process required for each project.

Chinese philosopher Lao Tzu famously said, "A journey of a thousand miles begins with one step." Just as a long journey starts with little steps, completing a big project requires starting with many small tasks. Breaking a large project down into smaller pieces makes it more manageable and easier to start. The busyness of family life can make it challenging to understand what should be done. Family members want a home that runs smoothly, but they need a better understanding of where to get started and what to do.

> *A journey of a thousand miles begins with one step.*
> *–Lao Tzu, Chinese philosopher and writer*

Clearly identifying and communicating the work to be accomplished at home relieves stress for both kids and parents. When there's a thorough plan, family members don't have to worry about missing a task. Instead, they can focus on getting the work done. Project management provides the structure for clear communication through documentation of the individual tasks that make up a project.

> ### *Document, distribute, and reinforce the work.*

The broad idea behind project management is to create a process to document, distribute, and reinforce the tasks to be completed. That's what we'll cover in the next three chapters. These chapters explain the nuts and bolts of task management, including identifying tasks, determining who does the work, and then managing it all to get the project done. You can apply these concepts to a project of any size at home, or even at work. In this chapter, we'll discuss how to gather, define, and document individual project tasks using examples of two relatively complicated projects that many families have to take on at some point: dealing with a medical situation and applying to college.

Identifying Tasks/Requirements Gathering

In the last chapter we looked at the first step of a project, the scoping phase, which involves understanding where you're going—that is, why you're undertaking the project and how you want it to look. The next step is to identify the specific tasks to be done. Let's use the example of dealing with a family member's health issues to see how identifying tasks can make things easier.

My husband and I know a lot about health problems, as between the two of us we've had more than 25 surgeries. He was born with a disability and spent a great deal of time in the hospital growing up. I have had numerous autoimmune issues and related complications. We also both have aging mothers with Parkinson's disease.

Project management has helped us, and can help you, deal with complicated medical situations, in part by clarifying what has to be done, which reduces stress. There's enough to worry about when a family member is sick, and by identifying necessary tasks, you can worry less about missing something and focus more on your sick loved one.

Any new medical problem can be daunting and scary. Knowing what's going to happen can ease the worry, and it's likely that there are other people who have gone through a similar situation. When my husband had surgery after we were married, I relied on his parents for information about his medical history, risks, and steps to aid in his recovery. In project management we know this type of historical information is valuable, and we use it to speed up the start of the next project and reduce duplication of work. Ask people if they have any recommendations: Does the doctor or hospital have a checklist of what has to be done? Are there relevant websites with information?

> ### *Don't reinvent the wheel—use previous projects for reference information.*

This same principle applies to any project. When beginning a new project, don't start from scratch. See if this type of project has been done before and if there are resources with useful information. To save yourself time, do a little research by talking to friends and family, perusing websites, reading books, etc.

Talk to other people impacted by the project, like relatives or friends, to see how they can help. Maybe they would be willing to help out around the house or organize meal delivery. For a health issue in the family, tell the children they can support the patient. Have a brainstorming session about what they can do to help the sick family member recover and write down everyone's ideas. Another option is to make it into a game and see who can write down the most suggestions. You can suggest small tasks like drawing the patient a picture or making them a meal. The kids will be glad to be involved, and their input could be quite valuable. Showing kids how they can take small steps toward helping the patient empowers them to handle a scary situation.

To get the most accurate information, involve experts who are assisting with the project—in this example, medical staff at the doctor's office. The experts have the most valuable information, so it's important to develop a positive relationship with them. Ask them detailed questions so you can capture all that has to be done and aren't surprised later. The research you've done beforehand will inform your preparations. Don't be afraid to ask a stupid question, because they probably have been asked it before.

Capturing Tasks—Meeting Notes

It's important to take notes during this process so you don't forget important details. Jot down your thoughts and take notes whether it's a meeting with your own family or with service providers or others outside your family. Meeting notes enable everyone to remember what was discussed and provide a reference to use later. They also allow people to read and clarify anything that might be confusing and hold people accountable for what they said they would do. In addition, family members who were unable to attend the meeting have a record of what happened. I use them for things like personal event planning, medical follow-ups, and school meetings. I think of meeting minutes as being a proactive way to clearly communicate, and they will probably produce a better outcome for your project. Written documentation gets people's attention because you have recorded what they committed to and you can refer to it to hold them accountable.

Here's an easy way to create useful notes. When you write them down during a meeting, divide them into two sections:

1. Items discussed
2. Next steps/follow-ups with the people responsible for each item

During the meeting, if a task is mentioned, note it, ask who will get it done, and make sure that you get everyone's email address if the meeting involves people outside of your family. Copy the content into an email and edit it for brevity. Begin and end with a thank you and tell people to let you know if they have any changes. If you're working on a computer, print out a copy so you can follow up on next steps.

Here's an example from a care plan meeting with my mother's medical team at a rehab center (names have been changed for confidentiality):

Dear Regina,

Thank you for organizing our mom's care plan meeting today.

Our main priorities are increasing her activity level and caloric intake so that she can perform the activities of daily living and return to her apartment.

Below are the follow-up items I captured.

Follow-ups:

1. Jon, OT, to request a speech screening due to slurred speech.

2. Regina, social worker, will schedule follow-up care plan meeting.

3. Laura, dietician, will discuss with mom alternate food options and food preferences.

Thanks Regina, and please let us know if you have any changes or updates. We look forward to hearing from you and the staff soon.

Best,

Hilary Kinney

Once the email is sent, use it to follow up on the outstanding items. Forward it the next week to the person responsible and ask them for an update and a timeline for when their task will be completed. Because you sent them the tasks the previous week, people can be held accountable and reminded of the tasks they previously committed to.

Now that you have recorded project information from experts, family members, and/or meetings, you can start breaking the project down into smaller tasks.

Task Definition

A task is an individual piece of work that's part of the larger project—one step in a long journey. The project needs to be broken down into small pieces that can be assigned to one person, clearly defined, and tracked. Make sure each task is precise, possible to complete in a short amount of time, and measurable, meaning it has a distinct starting and ending point. Generally speaking, you should be able to describe a task in one sentence.

It can be especially difficult for children to understand where to start on a big project. Adults need to help them break it down into actionable steps that may be smaller than adults are used to. Think about the appropriate length of time for a task depending on your child's age. Generally, younger children are better able to complete shorter tasks, while older children can handle longer ones. A way to illustrate tasks to little kids is to describe them as building blocks; each task is one block in a house that they're building. You start with the blocks on the bottom and add more blocks row by row until you have completed the house.

> *A task is a building block of the project.*

For example, a task like "recover from surgery" is too big and vague. Instead, focus on more specific tasks, such as "walk ten minutes every day" or "do physical therapy once a week." It can be useful to think through the sequential timeline of the project and what happens in what order. Write down each task that you think of, keeping in mind that additional tasks and details can be added later.

Not only do you need to know what must be done, you have to know how long it will take and how much it will cost. To determine the length or duration of a task, ask the other people involved:

1. What's the shortest time it can take?
2. What's the longest time it can take?
3. How much time is it most likely to take?

If you don't ask these three questions, they will likely default to the shortest estimate because that's what they assume you want to hear. Once you get the shortest, longest, and most realistic time estimates, you can decide how much time you want to build into the plan for this task. For example, my husband usually recovers faster from surgery than I do. Because we know this, we can factor it into our recovery plan and estimate shorter recovery times for him and longer ones for me.

> *For time and cost estimates, get three inputs: smallest, largest, and most realistic.*

For cost estimates, use the same approach as for time estimates and get a variety of perspectives from informed individuals. Obtain at least three estimates from three different providers and you'll have a clearer understanding of options.

Obtaining all the quotes before you commit to one provider makes it easier to make a sound decision.

Task Types

Tasks can be categorized in several ways: one-time, recurring, dependent, and parallel.

- **One-time task**—happens once
- **Recurring task**—happens more than once
- **Dependent task**—happens after a previous task
- **Parallel task**—happens at the same time as another task

One-time tasks can happen at any time and are completed individually. Recurring tasks happen once and then repeat later. Dependent tasks don't happen until the task before it has been completed, and parallel tasks happen along with another task. Here's a picture of what these tasks look like over time.

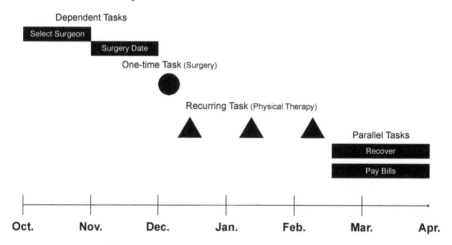

In our medical example, dependent tasks would include first selecting a surgeon and then scheduling the surgery date. The surgery itself would be a one-time task, while physical therapy would most likely be recurring. Parallel tasks would be things like paying medical bills and various recovery-related tasks.

Documenting Action Items

Once you have collected background information and identified the types of tasks needed, you can document them in one place for reference when managing the project. This ensures tasks aren't lost or forgotten. There are two categories of tracking systems: a list or a visual representation. Each of these options can be as complex as you wish, although I recommend using the least complicated tracking system that still adequately supports each project. Remember that the project management process you're using should add value and, in the long run, decrease the amount of work you're doing by keeping you better organized.

Small projects require less support, while larger, more complex projects require more. Project size is determined by the number of people involved and the amount of money and work required. Small projects, like organizing chores, have a limited number of tasks and don't require a lot of oversight or involve people outside the family. Medium projects, like planning an event, require more support to keep track of what has to happen. Large projects, like applying to college, involve multiple people outside the home and numerous different tasks. Here are the tracking options in increasing levels of complexity, first for a list format and then for a visual representation.

Lists of Tasks:

Small Projects:
- Sticky Notes
- Whiteboard
- Sheet of Paper
- Reminder list on phone

Medium to Large Projects:
- Spreadsheet List
- Action Item List sorted by category, date, and person responsible
- Task Management App

For smaller projects, lists can be enough to keep track of tasks. The simplest way to manage a small number of tasks is to put them on a sticky note, place it where you can see it, and throw it out when the tasks are done. A better option for a larger number of tasks is to use a list or bullet format on a whiteboard or sheet of paper. You can use pen and paper or document it on your computer. You can also use reminders on your smartphone, which has the added benefit of letting you add alerts. All of these options work for smaller projects that don't require a lot of management or communication outside the household.

For medium to large projects, tasks are easier to manage if they're organized in one place and distributed to the people involved. This can be done in a spreadsheet or using a task management app. Spreadsheet programs like Excel are useful because you can use them to easily sort and update items. Here's an example of an action item list that has several columns of information: status, task, category, owner, due date, and notes.

- Status—identifies the task as in progress, complete, ongoing, or on hold
- Task—describes the work to be done
- Category—groups tasks, like preparation and post-surgery (optional)
- Owner—identifies who is responsible for completing that task
- Due Date—the date when the task should be completed
- Notes—any clarifications about that task

Action Item List, Jeff's Surgery

Project Name: Jeff's Surgery					
STATUS	TASK	CATEGORY	OWNER	DUE DATE	Notes:
Complete	Select surgeon	Preparation	Jeff		
In Progress	Determine surgery date	Preparation	Jeff		Non-holiday weekend
Complete	Find babysitter for surgery day	Preparation	Hilary		
Planned	Travel from Wisconsin	Surgery	Jim		
Planned	Drive Jeff to hospital	Surgery	Jim		
Planned	Drive Jeff home post-surgery	Surgery	Hilary		
Planned	Ensure correct insurance billing	Post-surgery	Hilary		
Planned	Schedule physical therapy	Post-surgery	Hilary		

For a task list, the best place to start is listing all tasks you've already identified in the task column, then add more tasks as they come to mind. If a task seems too big, break it down into smaller ones. If you know who's responsible for it, then add their name. If you don't know who's doing it yet, write down the task so you don't forget it and add someone's name later. Keep in mind that this is a working document that will grow and change, so start with a draft and gradually add more information over time. Once you have a solid list of tasks that represent the whole project, you can move on to the other columns on the spreadsheet.

I group tasks into categories so they're easier to find and understand. For a surgery action item list, I would use categories such as Preparation, Surgery, and Post-surgery. This allows me to sort all the items in each category and focus on one section at a time. Although you might not know when every task has to be done, put in as many dates as you can so you get a sense of the overall timeline. For example, if you know that the surgery is in mid-April and recovery takes six weeks, then you know the return-to-work date will be early June.

Continually update your task list with more detailed information as the project goes along, which will help you remember what has to be done. It's useful to review the list with the family to talk through any updates or add new information. These spreadsheets can be shared via cloud-based services (Google Docs, DropBox, Microsoft Office, etc.) and status updates can be added from various locations.

Task management apps are another tool you may find useful. These apps use the same general information: task name, date due, and person responsible. They also can be used to assign tasks to various people and notify them on their phones. Task management apps can be especially useful when family or project team members don't live close to each other. For example, my sisters and I used an app when we were handling different tasks related to my Mom's medical issues despite living far apart from each other. Specific task management apps are covered in Chapter 8.

Visual Representation of Tasks:
- Work Breakdown Structure
- Timeline

Visual representations show the project as a whole and are a good way to summarize the large pieces of work. They clearly communicate the big picture and can be easier to understand than lots of text. These tools are more time-consuming to put together, so I only recommend them for more complex projects.

Two particularly useful visuals are a work breakdown structure (WBS) and a timeline. A WBS illustrates the work to be done, whereas a timeline focuses on dates. A WBS shows the work in categories so you can see which tasks are grouped together. By contrast, a timeline looks like a horizontal bar chart and shows how the major pieces of work will be completed over time. Which format will work best depends on whether your project is driven by specific tasks or dates.

Work Breakdown Structure

I generally prefer a WBS because it's shorter, easier to put together, and easier to understand. To create a WBS, think of the different large groups of tasks for your project. You can use as many categories as you want, but I recommend keeping them to one page. Place each task group in a box at the top across the page and list the large tasks beneath each task group. For a surgery, the large task groups would include Preparation, Surgery, and Post-surgery. The sequence of the groups would be listed from left to right. Below each of these categories, list the tasks to be completed with the person responsible for each. You can create a WBS in Microsoft Word by using a SmartArt graphic in list format. Here's an example:

Work Breakdown Structure, Jeff's Surgery

Preparation	Surgery	Post-Surgery
•Select surgeon (Jeff) •Determine date (Jeff) •Find kids babysitter for surgery day (Hilary) •Complete medical tests (Jeff)	•Drive Jeff to hospital (Jim) •Drop kids at babysitter (Hilary) •On-site at hospital AM (Hilary) •On-site at hospital PM (Jim)	•Drive Jeff home (Hilary) •Draw Dad a picture (Jr.) •Schedule physical therapy (Jim) •Pay medical bills (Hilary) •Rest and recover! (Jeff)

You also can add deadlines for each task or add timing for each group of work: Preparation (March/April), Surgery (April), Post-surgery (May/June).

This one-page summary of your entire project can be easily understood and tracked. You can also print it and post it in the kitchen for the entire family to refer to. When an item is completed, place a checkmark next to that task. This is an easy way to manage a project in one place.

The WBS can be used along with an action item list to provide more detail about specific tasks—for example, it would be useful to have a list of upcoming medical appointments for a surgery WBS. If the project doesn't have a lot of detailed tasks, a WBS by itself can be enough to manage the entire project.

Timeline

Timelines look like a horizontal bar chart and show the project plan over time. These visual representations are useful for projects that have important deadlines to keep track of. The length of the bar denotes how long each task will take. This format also shows how tasks may overlap. Dates are listed on the horizontal axis, and a vertical line can be used to show the present date. Here's an example created using shapes in Microsoft Word.

Timeline, Jeff's Surgery

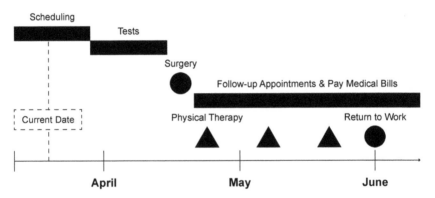

You can choose which of these tools you want to use for each project based on the project's level of complexity and your comfort level. I recommend going with the simplest solution as the project management should not take more time than the project itself!

Example: College Application Process

To help a child select and apply to a college, families can use the task identification and documentation process from start to finish. At the beginning of the process, the parents and their son do some research by talking with friends, reading books, and looking online. Next the parents discuss the overall process with their son and determine how much responsibility he will take on for the planning and task management. They decide that he will take on most of it with Mom's assistance.

Regular meetings are scheduled with the school college counselor. During these meetings, their son takes notes and emails the recap and next steps to the teachers and coaches involved. Mom guides him in developing an action item list for these tasks.

While learning about the required work, he adds tasks to the action item list on a spreadsheet. He determines the big work categories—College List, Visits, Application, Selection—and adds them to the category column. He then discusses milestones with his mom to build out the timeline. Since college application deadlines are in March, he has to finish visits by January and notes that date in the action item list. He then sets October as the deadline for determining the final list of colleges he wants to visit. He adds more information to the action item list later as it becomes available, including application due dates.

Action Item List, College Application Process

Project Name: College Application Process					
STATUS	TASK	CATEGORY	OWNER	DUE DATE	Notes:
Complete	Determine school preferences	College List	Jamal	30-Aug	Large University
In Progress	Research financial aid	College List	Dad	30-Sep	
In Progress	Determine final list of eight colleges	College List	Jamal	1-Oct	
In Progress	Plan college visit itinerary	Visits	Mom	20-Oct	
	Finish college visits	Visits	Jamal	30-Dec	
	Submit applications	Applications	Jamal	15-Mar	
	Rank acceptance list	Selection	All	30-Apr	

Next, with his mom, he creates a WBS so that they can see the entire project at once. He uses the same four categories as he did on the action item list—College List, Visits, Application, and Selection—and lists the larger tasks below each category pulled from the action item list.

Work Breakdown Structure, College Application Process

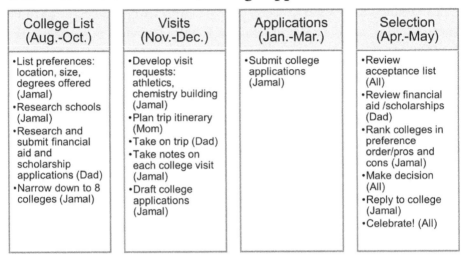

College List (Aug.-Oct.)	Visits (Nov.-Dec.)	Applications (Jan.-Mar.)	Selection (Apr.-May)
•List preferences: location, size, degrees offered (Jamal) •Research schools (Jamal) •Research and submit financial aid and scholarship applications (Dad) •Narrow down to 8 colleges (Jamal)	•Develop visit requests: athletics, chemistry building (Jamal) •Plan trip itinerary (Mom) •Take on trip (Dad) •Take notes on each college visit (Jamal) •Draft college applications (Jamal)	•Submit college applications (Jamal)	•Review acceptance list (All) •Review financial aid /scholarships (Dad) •Rank colleges in preference order/pros and cons (Jamal) •Make decision (All) •Reply to college (Jamal) •Celebrate! (All)

He decides that he also wants to use the timeline format and creates a simple chart to see progression and due dates.

Timeline, College Application Process

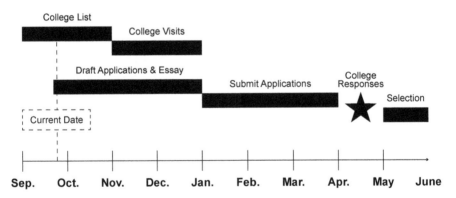

With these tools in place, they review the action items, timeline, and WBS weekly during their family meetings to manage the college application process and meet the deadlines.

Using these examples, you can start identifying, documenting, and visualizing different types of tasks in your family projects. With any project, I recommend using the simplest documentation. If you just want to use a list of bullets or a WBS, that's fine, and don't overengineer the supporting processes if it detracts from getting the work done. If the project is more complicated and you have to be able to sort tasks, use an action item list in a spreadsheet. Do what works for you. The next chapter covers resource capacity planning to further identify who does what work on these tasks.

Exercises

Exercise #1: Action Item List

Fill in this action item list for a project. Write down as many tasks as you can.

STATUS	TASK	CATEGORY	OWNER	DUE DATE	Notes:

Chapter 7
Knowing Who Does What When: Resource Capacity Planning and Maximizing Productivity

TOP TIPS TO KNOW WHO DOES WHAT WHEN:

1. Involve the family in determining and assigning the work around the house.

2. Get a view of each family member's schedule availability.

3. Document and display tasks so that everyone can remember the schedule.

Now that you know how to identify the work you want to get done, it's beneficial to clarify who does what. How do you decide which family member tackles which part of the work? This is often a sore spot, as some people may believe they're doing more than others. Although it may not solve all family disagreements on this issue, taking a more practical look at the overall workload and balancing it among family members can settle disputes and prevent hard feelings.

Project managers are constantly juggling resources to see how we can get everything accomplished. Who can work on our project, do they have the right skills, and are they available? We're competing with their other responsibilities, and they may have higher-priority projects that get more of their attention. Project managers also oversee several projects at the same time and share the workload with their fellow project managers. This sounds a lot like life at home, where family members have competing priorities and parents oversee the work. This is where project management can provide a neutral look at tasks and remove the emotion from the discussion. By looking at the task assignments objectively, the family can more clearly see everyone's capacity and agree to a fair distribution of work.

"Resource capacity planning" is a fancy term for figuring out who is available to do the work. It takes people's current assignments into consideration to weigh whether there's room in their schedule to take on something else. It also shows whether current work should have a lower or higher priority. The goal is ensuring that each person has an even workload throughout the year without spikes caused by an overloaded schedule.

The benefit of resource capacity planning is that, once you've assigned the work, the amount of mental space you have to dedicate to keeping track of it diminishes. Organizing housework and other chores leaves you more time to think about other things. You'll also distribute the work more evenly, which will reduce stress and the risk of burnout for an individual who is doing too much. In this chapter, we'll look at how to fairly identify who should do which jobs around the house. Then we'll cover how to maximize productivity with task-type management.

The Role of the Project Manager

One of the parents' roles is to plan, facilitate, and oversee the work to be done at home. This is commonly known as the "mental load" and is similar to a project manager's role in the corporate world. This project management role at home is often assumed by women and can become a source of frustration in families. Women in particular can become burned out if they are doing all of this extra organizing work to keep the household on track and are not recognized for their efforts. What would happen if this project management work did not get done at home? Chores would not happen, the kids would not get picked up from activities, there would be no groceries in the pantry, and there would be confusion about what needed to happen next.

> ### *How are you going to fill the project management role in your family?*

How are you going to fill the project management role in your family? Although the job can be done by one person, it often works best for parents to share the load and oversee different areas, such as schoolwork, chores, meals/groceries, bills, etc. How much of this project management work each parent does will depend on their other responsibilities. For example, one parent could oversee several areas if the other parent is busy with another project, and then they could make adjustments when circumstances change. If something new pops up, like vacation planning, talk about who wants to handle that project or parts of it. My husband and I use this flexible approach; depending on what is going on with our jobs, our roles around the house may change. Discuss what work has to be done and look at everyone's schedules to determine the project manager roles in your home.

Resource Capacity Planning—Weekly

To get a picture of each family member's availability, give them a chart like the one below to fill out their daily schedule. Include the parts of their day that take up large chunks of time, like sleeping, dressing, eating, work, school, commuting, recreational activities, homework, exercise, chores, time with family and friends, etc. If some people are already spending a significant amount of time on chores, list them. Have each family member fill out the hours spent per day on each item and add up the totals for each day of the week. Have each person share their results and see who has some extra time.

If your family isn't inclined to fill out a weekly chart, I get it; it is a detailed, time-consuming exercise. Instead, have a conversation about their schedule and when they're available during the week.

Let's look at the theory behind this exercise, because it will help you apply it, whether in a conversation or on paper. As we all know, much of our day is taken up by things such as sleep and work. Let's put those big blocks of time in the chart below first. If it's easier, bundle fundamental items like sleeping, eating, and getting dressed together in one number. Below is an example of what a weekly chart might look like. Your situation will be different, of course, so add and subtract categories as needed.

Mom Hours/Day	Mon	Tue	Wed	Thu	Fri	Sat	Sun
Sleep	8	8	8	8	8	8	8
Prep AM & PM (Dress/Eat)	2	2	2	2	2	2	2
Work/School + Commute	9	9	9	9	9		
Extracurricular Activities						2	2
Grandma Care			2			3	
Homework	--	--	--	--	--	--	--
Exercise			.5			.5	
Chores	.5	.5	1	.5	1.5	2	
Meal Prep	1	1	1	1	1	1	1
Dishes	.25	.25	.25	.25	.25	.25	.25
Family/Friends Time	.5	.5	.5	.5	.5	2	2
Total	21	21	24.25	21.25	22.25	21.25	15.75

This type of analysis will show each person's current schedule. So if one family member has a long commute to work or school, that will cut into their availability to do family-related work. If one child has a lot of homework or extracurricular activities, that will limit their availability. Knowing which days of the week are busiest for people can help when scheduling additional activities. For example, if Mom is overscheduled on Wednesdays, it's probably not a good idea to sign Junior up for soccer on that day.

This exercise also helps you reexamine your priorities from the stop sign exercise and can help you decide whether you need to change the amount of time spent on certain activities. Is your family spending enough time on the most important priorities, or are other items sneaking into the family schedule? Are you getting enough sleep, exercise, and time with family and friends? If not, consider spending less time on other things. Should your kids revisit their priorities? For example, your child may think a "higher-priority" project is their social media feed or time with friends rather than homework.

Resource Capacity Planning—Seasonal

Also consider seasonal capacity planning to ensure that the schedule stays as balanced as possible over the entire year. Think about how the family's workload will change throughout the year. For example, back-to-school time in the fall and winter holidays are often the busiest times of year for many families. Certain professions have busier times, such as accountants during budget season or teachers during the school year. On the other hand, summers may slow down for the kids when school is out of session.

Keep these seasonal fluctuations in mind as you consider your broader family schedule and try to schedule major projects and activities for the slower times. For instance, a winter sport may be difficult to manage with all the other holiday activities happening, so find one that starts in January instead of December. Try to keep an even workload throughout the year to prevent stress and burnout.

Shared Calendar

A shared calendar can be invaluable for keeping track of the family schedule and helping family members communicate about what's happening each day. Although a paper calendar on the kitchen wall will do, I find mobile apps to be the most useful because you can check them on the go from your smartphone. These apps also list participants, and they can send reminders about each activity. Parents can assign activities to each other to keep track of who is doing what that day, like pickup. As kids get older, they can enter their own activities on the shared family calendar.

There are many shared calendar apps to choose from, including Alarmed, Cozi, Google Calendar, Picniic, S'mores Up, and others. Some of these apps also include task management and incentive systems. A shared calendar is an effective starting discussion point for the weekly family meeting to review what's happening in the coming week and whether any adjustments should be made.

Family-Related Work

Now that we know the family schedule, let's figure out who can help out around the house. There's a lot to do to keep the family running, like cooking and cleaning. I call this family-related work. This work is the area that requires the most attention because the entire family can be involved in it. Much of our other work is mostly individual and can't be shared. For example, we can't go to school with our kids, and our kids can't do our work at the office. Let's analyze family-related work and who should do which tasks.

First, let's look at some of the things that make the family run:

- Animal care
- Change bedsheets
- Clean bathrooms
- Clean kitchen
- Cooking
- Dishes
- Dry cleaning
- Dusting
- Grocery shopping
- House maintenance
- Laundry
- Mop floors
- Pay bills
- Pick up bedroom
- Pick up shared living areas
- Schedule Drs. appts.
- Schedule lessons and activities
- Set the table
- Sweep floors
- Take out recycling
- Take out trash
- Vacuum
- Yardwork
- Water plants
- Window cleaning

It's useful for the entire family to be aware of all the work that has to be done around the house, so step number one is to discuss it. Have a brainstorming session and ask each person to contribute their ideas on a sheet of paper or on sticky notes. You can make it a game to see who can write down the most chores or tasks. This exercise ensures that responsibilities are captured and the family understands the different tasks and appreciates the amount of work required.

Once you know what has to be done, how do you decide who should do which jobs? Having the overall picture of what people are doing currently provides the background to make decisions. You can get a snapshot of people's schedules by discussing it or asking them to fill out the detailed weekly chart of what they are spending their time on currently. Then you'll be able to compare schedules, discuss time management, and see what makes sense for dividing up the family-related work.

Assigning Family-Related Work

With this reference of schedule availability, you can assign chores by looking at capacity and preference across the family. First look at the master list of all the chores that have to be done at your house, which you created together. Then sit down with the family and start figuring out who does what. You can start by asking if there are any tasks someone would like to do because they have a natural interest in it. They would have the first choice to do that task. If there are chores that no one wants to do, like take out the trash, you can see who has the capacity to do it based on the charts and assign it that way. You could also rotate the less desirable chores. If you want to add a little fun to the exercise, place each chore on a piece of paper in a bowl and have a person pick out a chore to add to their list.

Once you know who will do each chore, you can list them on a weekly schedule to see the tasks and how they compare to availability. You can always revisit this plan later, but let the family know you'll start with this schedule and then adjust it if necessary. Putting it on paper shows people how the work is distributed, holds everyone accountable, and is a useful reminder. A chore chart can be a poster board, whiteboard, chalkboard, or spreadsheet. Post it in an area where everyone can see it and refer to it. In the next chapter, I'll cover how to combine the chore chart with schoolwork, if necessary.

Here is an example of a weekly chore chart:

	Daily	Mon	Tue	Wed	Thu	Fri	Sat	Sun
Mom	Cook dinner		Change bedsheets	Vacuum upstairs	Clean bathroom	Kids' laundry	Groceries, Vacuum & Mop downstairs	Cooking Prep
Dad	Clean kitchen	Parents' laundry					Vacuum, Clean bathroom	Yardwork
Jamal	Set table, Empty dishwasher	Trash	Recycling				Clean bathroom Clean bedroom	Help with cooking

Jane	Walk dog			Clean bath-room		Sweep stairs and foyer	Dust and neaten, Clean bed-room	Assist with yard-work

Listing all chores on a weekly schedule for the entire family (including the parents) removes the stress of wondering what has to be done, who's going to do it, and when. Add a column for daily tasks so that everyone is clear about what's expected of them. Chores are easiest to remember if they occur on the same day every week. So, if the bathroom should be cleaned once a week, just note that it will be done on Thursdays. This helps everyone remember it and reduces nagging because the expectation has been set.

I would also recommend rotating chores so that all family members can understand the work and the impact they have on it. If they are assigned to neaten up the living room, then they will be less apt to make it messy. If they make dinner, they will realize that they want everyone to show up on time. Rotating chores puts them in other people's shoes and hopefully makes them more understanding and considerate. In the next chapter we'll discuss how to make chores more fun through gamification; in the meantime, let's focus on how to get them done more quickly!

Maximizing Productivity

Everyone wants to be more efficient. For me, housecleaning and laundry are my least favorite tasks to do around the house; I would much rather do yardwork or cooking. People have preferences for what tasks they enjoy; as for the rest, let's get them done as quickly as possible.

A concept called "task-type management" helps determine what you work on when. As we discussed in Chapter 6, tasks can be categorized in several ways: one-time, recurring, dependent, and parallel. You can speed up how fast tasks are completed by how you organize them. **One-time tasks** can happen at any time and are completed individually. **Recurring tasks** happen once and then repeat later. **Dependent tasks** don't happen until the task before it is complete, and **parallel tasks** happen along with another task at the same time. An additional type of task is called **batching**, where you complete multiples of the same task at the same time. Finally, **automated tasks** are those that can be made easier through technology, subscription services, and other methods. With these categories in mind, you can rearrange various tasks to get the most done in the most efficient way.

- One-time task—How many can you get done and check off the list?
- Recurring task—How much faster and more efficiently can you complete the task over time?
- Dependent task—How quickly can you get it started when the preceding task is done?
- Parallel task—What different tasks can you get done at the same time?
- Batching tasks—How many can you get done at once?
- Automated tasks—What can be set up and scheduled to occur routinely?

One-time tasks can usually be checked off relatively quickly; I find these the most satisfying to complete because they're "one and done." Make yourself a list and try to complete as many as possible for a sense of accomplishment. A chalkboard in the kitchen or a list of reminders on your phone is a good place to keep track of one-time tasks. Look for tasks that are similar and do them at the same time. For example, if you have several phone calls to make, get them all done in a row.

Recurring tasks are done regularly, like vacuuming and yard work. Because these are repetitive, you can get better and better at them over time. Challenge the kids to figure out how quickly they can complete a recurring task (while still doing it well). What can they do differently to make it easier? For example, could they move the furniture a certain way to vacuum or mow the lawn in a particular pattern that's most efficient?

Dependent tasks are the most difficult and require more planning. If you forget about a task that other tasks depend on, you can get stuck—for example, when there are wet bedsheets in the washer that haven't been put in the dryer and it's time to go to bed, or when it's the morning of a basketball game and my son's jersey is still dirty from the last game. To avoid these situations, use a calendar or reminders list and mark what is to be done on what day, so you don't forget it—e.g., "wash basketball uniform on Wednesday." Dependent tasks can be especially useful in meal planning to get dinner on the table faster. For example, cook meats or pasta in advance and warm it up at dinner time, or prepare the entire casserole in advance and refrigerate it until it is time to cook for dinner.

My favorite trick is to use **parallel tasks** to be more efficient. What can you do simultaneously and get twice as much done at once? For example, your child can watch TV and fold laundry at the same time or get some exercise while taking the dog for a walk. You can make dinner while helping your child with their homework, buy groceries while your child is at soccer practice, take a conference call during your commute, or schedule a doctor's appointment while waiting in the car to pick up your kids at school.

Another way to consider tasks is **batching**, which involves doing the same task multiple times at the same time. For example, you can make several of the same meal and freeze or refrigerate some of the food. My son likes omelets, so I make two or three at once and put them in the fridge for a few days. This means less time in the kitchen and fewer dishes to clean. Along the same lines, you could buy items in bulk so you don't have to go to the store as often. Batching is useful for items that can be stored and used later.

Also consider setting up **automated tasks** to get them done easier and faster. This involves using technology to schedule or set up something to occur on its own without you directly managing it each time. For example, you could invest in a robotic vacuum or lawn mower or set up automated bill payments through your bank or subscription deliveries. These automated tasks may be more expensive, so you'll have to see if they fit into the family budget.

Before you tackle your task list, think about which types of tasks they are and how you can manage their distinct characteristics to get more done.

Master Task Lists

If a series of more complex tasks are repeated on a regular basis, document them on a master task list to refer to later, which saves time and energy. Examples could be grocery lists, meal planning, housecleaning, birthday party preparations, daily care plans, etc. A master task list can be notes on a piece of paper on the fridge, a list on your phone, or a spreadsheet that can be edited and printed each week.

For meal planning, keep a list of the family's favorite meals, which will make it easier to come up with dinner ideas. My sister calls it their "Greatest Hits" and asks the family which hits they want to eat that week. You could also keep a list of the ingredients, so you know what to buy at the grocery store for each dish. In addition, your grocery list has items that you buy regularly, so keep a master list for reference. This will record key items and save a return trip to the store.

Listing the different steps to complete a task can be useful for little kids who may not know where to start. If their job is to clean up the playroom, post a list of smaller tasks on the playroom wall for them to follow—e.g., put Legos in orange bin, put books on a shelf, put train tracks in clear bin. For cleaning their bedroom, the list may include picking up items on the floor and stripping the bed linens and putting them in the washer. The kids will be empowered to complete the tasks correctly, require less supervision, and be more independent.

The master task list can also be useful for people outside the family. I was in this situation with my mother's caregivers. She had multiple caregivers at home who would vary from week to week, and at first, they didn't understand my mom's needs and desires. It became a source of frustration to visit and see that things weren't happening like we thought they should be. So I documented a daily care plan for each caregiver shift. I then asked my mom, sisters, and the caregiver agency to review it, and I updated it with their input. I posted the final plan in my mom's apartment and discussed it with the healthcare aides. We reinforced it by checking that it was being followed when we went to visit and by asking my mom if her needs were being met. If the tasks weren't being completed, we reminded the caregivers of the list and informed the agency of our expectations for accountability. The daily care plan provided a sustainable, long-term framework to manage my mom's care, regardless of which caregivers were on duty. Overall, the care plan reduced our workload and frustration, improved my mom's care, and fostered peace of mind.

For tasks or processes that are done repeatedly, keep a record of the steps so that people can complete the task independently, reduce mistakes, improve quality, and save time.

Example: Assigning Chores

Mom is overwhelmed and exhausted, and the family is having arguments about who should do which chores around the house. To address this, they all sit down and brainstorm the work that has to happen around the house. They make it a game, and whoever writes the most ideas on sticky notes wins a chocolate bar. They all realize how much work it is and decided to buy a robotic vacuum and set up automated bills to reduce the workload.

Then each family member fills out their weekly schedule to see what their days look like. Dad realizes that Mom was taking on a lot of the mental load as the project manager and agrees to oversee bills and chores. They find out that Junior is spending two hours per day playing video games and decide that he can do more chores around the house.

To divide up the work, the family first volunteers for chores that they are interested in. Then, using the list of the rest of the chores, they fill in the chore chart. Chores that no one wants to do are written on a piece of paper, and each person picks one from a bowl. Dad then starts reminding the kids to get the chores done, and on Saturdays, they hold contests to see who can get their chores done the fastest. They celebrate with ice cream when all the chores get done for the week.

Resource capacity planning can relieve a lot of the arguments about who does what around the house. Family members better understand the amount of work required and can support each other. By knowing what's involved and the capacity of each person, work can be more evenly distributed and shared. These ideas will help you enjoy a more peaceful home in which family members understand the work involved, communication improves, the kids feel empowered, the parents are less stressed, and the family succeeds as a team.

Exercises

Exercise #1: Chore Brainstorming Session

Have a brainstorming session with the family to list all the chores that must be done around the house, including the work of the project manager. Have them write each one on a sticky note and post it on the wall or list them on a sheet of paper. Make it a contest and to see who generates the most chores.

Exercise #2: Weekly Schedule Analysis

Have each family member fill out their weekly schedule, and then share and discuss it with the entire family.

Hours/Day	Mon	Tue	Wed	Thu	Fri	Sat	Sun
Sleep							
Prep AM & PM (Dress/Eat)							
Work/School + Commute							
Extracurricular Activities							
Homework							
Exercise							
Chores							
Meal Prep							
Dishes							
Family/Friends							
Total							

Exercise #3: Chore Assignments

Assign chores by first asking if there are chores anyone would prefer to do; then assign the rest of the chores based on capacity.

Exercise #4: Chore Chart

Make a weekly chore chart that includes items for the kids and parents or add the chores to the task lists that will be covered in the next chapter.

Chapter 8
GETTING IT DONE: ORGANIZING ACTION ITEMS AND MOTIVATING THE KIDS

TOP TIPS FOR GETTING IT DONE:

. . . .

1. Keep it simple and use a tracking system that works for everyone.

2. Have regular meetings to check the status of work.

3. Make tasks fun with games and rewards.

. . . .

W
ould you like less nagging to get work done around the house and fewer questions from the kids about what they need to do every day? Although it may seem like a lot of work initially, setting up a task management system will pay off in the long run, and you can also make it fun!

We put these systems in place during the coronavirus pandemic while my son's school was online. They reduced interruptions to my husband's and my work and motivated my son to complete assignments on his own.-

Using one of the systems I've outlined below will help your family members clearly understand their responsibilities, and your kids will be able to better manage their own work. As a bonus, your kids will become more empowered and independent.

First, we'll discuss different family roles and responsibilities and review a selection of tracking tools, from simple to advanced. Then we'll talk about how gamification, targeted motivation, and oversight meetings keep tasks fun and on track.

Family Roles and Responsibilities

The project manager role of organizing and overseeing the work is filled by the parents, and the entire family helps with the work. Each family member should be responsible for completing their own tasks. Sometimes this is easier said than done. We can often be tempted to do work that our kids should do, whether that's chores, schoolwork, or something else. A project manager's role is to facilitate the work. If we jump in and do everything for our kids (or our spouses, for that matter), it just creates more work for us and prevents them from learning essential skills. We should provide every family member with training and support and then step back and allow them to practice.

The family engagement techniques we discussed earlier will facilitate getting things done. By involving the family members in the planning and explaining what's in it for them, they will have an incentive to participate. Plus, there will be less fighting and nagging—and we could all use some of that!

Task Management Tools

Children tend to get distracted easily, and for many of us adults juggling so many balls in the air, it is easy to get distracted too. I find that the best approach is to keep task management tools clear, simple, and easy to access.

You may need to use different communication techniques for each family member. Think about how your children learn and process information best. Are they visual, auditory, or hands-on learners? Use communication techniques that incorporate their preferred learning styles. If they're visual learners, use pictures or icons to illustrate tasks, like a picture of a book for reading. If they're auditory learners, tell them what they have to do. If they're more hands-on and tactile, have them manipulate objects like paper clips to show a task is complete. Are they a future project manager? Then give them a list to check off completed items.

There are a variety of task management tools to choose from: sheets of paper, whiteboards, calendars, spreadsheets, posters, or computer programs. The number of people in your family can determine which tools work best for you. A simple system, like a few sheets of paper, may be fine for a smaller family, while a larger family may require spreadsheets or task management software. Choose the least complex system that works for your family. The task management system should make life easier for you in the long run and be manageable for you and the family members. As kids get older, they can start documenting and managing their own tasks and select the system that works best for them.

Simple Task Management System

Monday
- Reading HW
- Math HW
- Take out trash
To Do This Week
- Art HW
- Music HW

As an example, consider schoolwork and chores. The simplest way to manage these tasks is to list each one on a whiteboard or piece of paper each day and hang it where your children can see and reach it. Then they can mark each task when it's complete. This system works best when the number of tasks is relatively small and many of them are recurring.

We used this approach when our son was in elementary school. I would write down his school assignments and chores for each day on a whiteboard, and we would erase each item when it was done. He loved erasing tasks when he was finished with them.

Tasks to be completed later in the week can be listed toward the bottom and completed as time allows. For example, my son had weekly art and music homework that I listed on the bottom of the whiteboard, and he would complete this work on days when there was less homework to do.

Intermediate Task Management System

Reference Sheet

When there are more tasks or children to keep track of, it's useful to keep a reference sheet for tasks that repeat. Use this reference sheet along with your preferred communication method, such as paper or a whiteboard. The reference sheet can be customized for each day of the week and/or each child. For example, math homework might be due Monday and Friday, while Thursdays might include laundry and a book report. Add these tasks to the whiteboard or piece of paper along with daily tasks.

This system worked for us when our child's homework became more complex and harder to keep track of. I kept a document of weekly recurring homework and pulled from it when compiling daily tasks on the whiteboard. This reference document listed all our son's homework that was regularly due for each subject. I also included chores, such as taking out the trash on Monday and recycling on Wednesday.

Binder or Workbook

If you have multiple children or a lot of schoolwork or activities, you might find it useful to keep a separate document for each child in a three-ring binder. List ongoing homework for each class and activity and refer to it to add to your daily task list.

Another option is to use a spreadsheet workbook with tabs for each day of the week. Each tab would list recurring tasks for that day. At the beginning of the week, print out the workbook and post each day individually, adding new tasks as needed. Different workbooks could be created for additional children.

Weekly Calendar

If you prefer not to write out what has to be done every day, you could use a weekly calendar format. This approach can be easier for visual learners to understand. For example, list all recurring tasks for each day of the week and print out the entire week at once. Leave enough room at the bottom of each day to add any new items. Note that kids may find it overwhelming to see all the work they have to do for the week, so you just could show one day at a time, to be more manageable for them.

Monday	Tuesday	Wednesday	Thursday	Friday	Saturday
- Reading HW - Math HW - Take out trash	- Reading HW - Math HW - Writing HW - Art HW due	- Reading HW - Math HW - Clean room - Recycling	- Reading HW - Math HW - Writing HW - Music HW	- Book report due - Reading HW - Math HW	- Clean bathroom - Sweep stairs

Advanced Task Management Systems

For larger families, a more advanced task management system may be clearer so you can see everything that's happening all at once.

Kanban Board

A Kanban board, similar to a bulletin board, shows all tasks in progress for everyone in the family. This is a great way to quickly see the status of all your kids' tasks at once and can be especially useful for larger families. Kanban boards can be created on a large whiteboard, chalkboard, poster board, felt board, or window, and sized according to the number of family members.

On a Kanban board, the workflow is shown from left to right across the top, and the people responsible for each task are shown along one side. The tasks are written down on sticky notes, and each note is moved from left to right across the board as a task progresses. Workflow stages written across the top include "To Do," "Doing," and "Done," while your kids' names are in rows on the left.

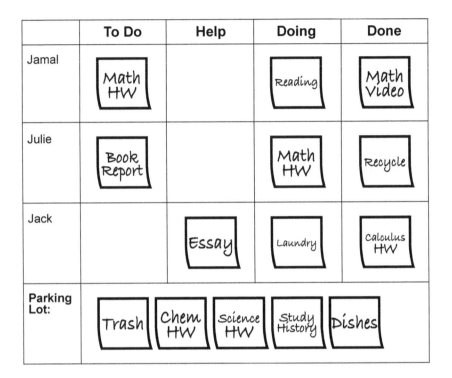

	To Do	Help	Doing	Done
Jamal	Math HW		Reading	Math Video
Julie	Book Report		Math HW	Recycle
Jack		Essay	Laundry	Calculus HW
Parking Lot:	Trash	Chem HW	Science HW	Study History	Dishes

Your kids write action items on sticky notes and move them from left to right across the board as they complete each stage. The "To Do" stage represents what they plan on doing that day, "Doing" includes tasks that are in progress, and "Done" includes completed tasks. A column labeled "Help" is used to identify work that someone finds difficult. This is useful because if a child gets stuck on something, he or she simply moves that task to the "Help" column and continues with another task until a parent has time to provide assistance. Finally, a "Parking Lot" column contains all the tasks that have to be accomplished for that week but haven't been started. Sticky notes with recurring tasks can be reused each week.

If you want, you can add a "Check" column before the "Done" column so you can review work and provide feedback. In addition, tasks can be color-coded by child or type (like homework or chores). For younger children, tasks can be shown as pictures instead of words, such as a book for reading or clothes for laundry.

Work Breakdown Structure

WBS, which was covered in Chapter 6, is useful for single projects so all the large categories of work can be seen at once. These could be used for a large science project or research assignment. They provide a one-page visual representation of the project from start to finish. These could be posted in one place so work can be checked off as it's completed. WBSs can be used along with an action item list to track smaller tasks.

Software and Apps

Older children can use more complex systems like task management software and apps. The same general task management concepts are applied, although they may have to be adapted to fit the program's interface. These software-based solutions can be a good option for more technically inclined families. These apps are especially useful when the members are living separately, like families of divorce, because people can see what is happening in one central location. As another example, when my sisters and I were downsizing my mother's home, we lived in different states. We used a task management app to update each other on new tasks and when we'd completed one.

There are many software options out there to choose from. Some that are geared toward families include Alarmed, Any.do, Habitica, Picniic, Remember The Milk, S'mores Up, Things 3, and ToDoist. Some of these apps also include incentive systems and gamification to make it more motivating for kids to accomplish tasks. For families that want advanced functionality like digital Kanban boards, apps like Asana, Bloo, ClickUp, Monday.com, and Trello are geared toward business but can be used for home projects as well.

Equipping Older Children to Manage Schoolwork Independently

As kids get older, they can use these tools to manage their own schoolwork, and you can equip them to make the transition. The end goal is for them to manage the three steps in the process independently: capture the assigned tasks, compile the tasks in one place, and manage the work to completion.

The first step is for your child to record what tasks have been assigned while they're at school. This can be done with a daily planner (the traditional paper version), a composition book or notepad, an app on their phone, or a spreadsheet. They can keep track of the work on their own, or they can incorporate their tasks into your family task management system (task list, Kanban board, calendar, app, etc.).

If they need help managing the work, walk them through the task identification process covered in Chapter 6. Have them tell you their assignments and discuss what has to be done and how long it will take. Next, break down the subtasks into manageable sizes and add these tasks to the family list, like the Kanban board. Now that the tasks are identified, review the task list with them regularly, cross off completed work, and talk through what should happen next.

Once your child has practiced identifying tasks and adding them to the master family list with you, have them do it themselves with you providing oversight. Then let them try the entire process (identifying subtasks, adding them to the master list, completing them) on their own for a week and be available for support. When they are ready, they can transition to their own system like an individual task list. Gradually give them more responsibility to be able to manage this end-to-end process themselves. These skills will serve them long-term at school, home, and work as they learn to tackle an assignment and manage the work from start to finish.

Gamification

As I said at the beginning of the book, all work and no play make for a dull family. So why don't we have fun and encourage kids to complete their tasks? Gamification is the idea of turning anything into a game to motivate participants. Now that we've organized the work to be done, here are a few ideas to turn work into play for the family:

1. First to the Finish—See which family member completes all their tasks the fastest for that week. (Make sure they know you'll check to see that they've done a thorough job!) Then that person gets to pick the reward for the entire family, like their favorite meal or family activity.

2. Countdown—Each person is given a room to clean and the first one to finish wins! (Again, let them know you'll be checking to make sure they've done a thorough job.) Each week see if the best time can be beaten.

3. Team Contest—Break the family into teams and assign items from the chore list. Compete to see which team finishes first.

4. Trade it—Each family member writes down one chore they don't want to do and places it in a bowl. One at a time, family members take one chore out of the bowl or steal one that someone has already opened.

After one round, the first player can swap their chore with anyone else; when someone does not want to trade, the game ends.

Keeping it fun makes the work go faster and bonds the family together while building teamwork.

Targeted Motivation

To keep the momentum going, there are specific ways to encourage kids to get work done by targeting rewards to tasks. There are many theories on motivating children, and here I'll explain how to apply whichever method you use to project management tools. Basically, what you'll do is assign value to tasks and then reward or penalize the child for completing or not completing the task. The values can be assigned based on size and length of task, or you can assign one value to every task. The values can be represented by points, stars, or game chips (tokens, poker chips, etc.), but I'll use points throughout this example. The child would be rewarded with points for completing a task or penalized by removing or not receiving points.

You can also add guidelines to the tasks for timeliness, quality of work, and proactiveness. Do you want your children to do the chores without being reminded, with a certain level of thoroughness, or by a certain date or time? For example, you could require that kids thoroughly complete all chores by Saturday at 4:00 p.m., without needing to be reminded. If they don't meet the requirement, then they wouldn't receive the points. They also could do extra chores for additional points or earn double points for a period of time—for example, to get the house cleaned quickly for an upcoming party.

Keep track of everyone's points with a poster board, whiteboard, chalkboard, or jar. For example, you could place a sticker or star on the poster board or add game chips to a jar. Rewards can be deferred for kids to save their points for something bigger. We've used different versions of these record-keeping systems in our family. When my son was younger, we used stars on a poster board. We've also used game chips in a jar, and now we keep track on a whiteboard.

Depending on what project management tools you use, you can add this rewards system to your chore chart, Kanban board, or task list. You can write the value next to each task, and then log it when completed.

Provide rewards when children complete their tasks. Think about what motivates your kids. Is it money, screen time, toys, privileges, an activity, or something else? Tie their rewards to these things. For example, you could provide your child with five minutes of screen time for each task they complete or a trip to the toy store or expanded privileges if they have a certain number of points. Another option you might explore is requiring your kids to complete all their chores for the week within the guidelines you've established as a condition of their allowance. Each kid is unique and may need different rewards, so figure out what works for your child. Changing it up can keep children motivated as you adapt to what interests them at the time. A trip to the dollar store may work for younger kids, then screen time, progressing to an allowance, and eventually privileges to use the car or go out with friends when they're older.

Oversight and Status Update Meetings

Once the task management and motivation plan is in place, it has to be managed and monitored by the parents or guardians. Parents can discuss it and decide who's in charge of which part of the plan. For example, one parent could be responsible for writing out the tasks and the other for checking on the status periodically. Or one parent could oversee and assign chores and the other parent oversee the schoolwork.

The key to making these systems work is having the daily discipline to keep them running. It may seem like more work, but managing the plan frees parents up to do other things and helps everyone remember what needs to be accomplished. It reduces the mental load for parents, plus the trash or recycling will be less apt to be forgotten, and the household tasks keep moving forward. As kids get older, they can manage more of the schoolwork themselves and don't require as much assistance.

Regular family meetings can also keep everyone focused on the work and provide structure. For schoolwork and chores, it may be useful to have daily check-in meetings. A short conversation over a meal can provide the opportunity to review the list, see if there are any questions, and allow the kids to ask for support if they need it. If you're using a Kanban board, a quick glance will tell you the status of the work, and you can ask questions about it. These daily meetings can be modeled after the weekly family meetings covered in Chapter 1 by asking three questions, based on the rose flower analogy:

1. What have you done/completed? What are your fully bloomed roses?
2. What do you need help with? What were your thorns this week?
3. What will you do/work on next? Where do you see new buds?

During these conversations, the family can make changes to the plan based on how it is going. For example, if the kids have lots of items in the "Help" column of the Kanban board, the parents can adjust their schedule to provide assistance. As kids get older, you could transition to less frequent or weekly meetings and check in with them on how school is going and whether they need support.

Committing to these processes will pay off in the long run, providing more peace at home and independence for the kids. The kids can choose which task to work on next and build their decision-making and executive-function skills. Kids will also have more ownership over their own work. Stick with it, and you'll see results.

Example: Holiday Planning

The holiday season is often the busiest time of year for parents, so here's how to use these task management processes to share the workload. First, hold a family meeting and discuss what work needs to be done and what fun events to include. Everyone can brainstorm and write down their ideas on sticky notes. Then each person can read their ideas out loud, like putting up outdoor decorations, writing holiday cards, making cookies, cleaning the house, cooking holiday dinner, having a party, and wrapping and shipping presents.

After the brainstorming session, the parents and older kids can review the ideas and split up large tasks into manageable pieces on new sticky notes. For example, making a holiday dinner can be broken down into creating menu, writing the shopping list, shopping for groceries, cooking the main dish, cooking the side dishes, making dessert, setting the table, and cleaning the kitchen.

Next, get together again to review the tasks and decide who is going to do what. Read each task and ask who would like to do it or share the job with another person. Write down on the sticky note which person signed up for that job.

Post the sticky notes on a Kanban Board with a piece of candy taped next to each task. When a task is completed, move it down the board and eat the candy! Over meals, review progress on holiday planning (what is going well, what people need help with, and what everyone will do next). When the holidays come, everyone can enjoy a more peaceful time together and take pride in their work.

Here is an example of a holiday-planning Kanban Board:

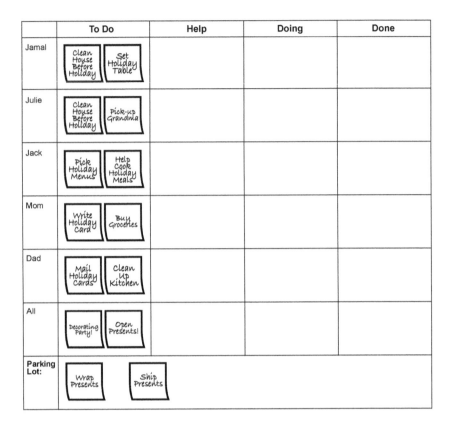

	To Do	Help	Doing	Done
Jamal	Clean House Before Holiday / Set Holiday Table			
Julie	Clean House Before Holiday / Pick-up Grandma			
Jack	Pick Holiday Menus / Help Cook Holiday Meals			
Mom	Write Holiday Card / Buy Groceries			
Dad	Mail Holiday Cards / Clean Up Kitchen			
All	Decorating Party! / Open Presents!			
Parking Lot:	Wrap Presents / Ship Presents			

Using these project management tools family members understand all the work involved, communication improves, the kids feel empowered, the parents are less stressed, and the family succeeds as a team.

Exercises

Exercise #1: Task Management System

Select a simple, intermediate, or advanced task management system for your family. Purchase the materials, put the system in place, and determine daily or weekly check-in times.

- Sheet of paper
- Whiteboard
- Calendar
- Spreadsheet
- Kanban Board
- Computer program or app

Chapter 9
Being Prepared: Managing Risk

TOP TIPS FOR MANAGING RISK:

· ·

1. Proactively consider risks to your family (especially teenagers).

2. Develop a risk management plan and implement as needed.

3. Revisit top risks at least once a year and update plans if necessary.

· ·

N ow that you know how to organize and accomplish the work, let's talk about being prepared for any unknowns that may happen along the way. No parent looks forward to days when school is cancelled because of snow or a childcare provider calls out sick. We are stretched thin already, and any unexpected changes to the schedule can be stressful and difficult to manage. Life is full of surprises, especially with kids, but project management has a process to anticipate and address them.

Risk is a valuable concept in project management and a proactive way to save you worry, time, and money. Project managers look at risk as something to identify and prepare for in advance. A risk is a possible event that could be a threat or opportunity for your family. The idea is to be ready if it happens. Project teams come up with a list of potential risks and develop a response plan. They consider risks throughout a project and regularly reevaluate them. This becomes an ongoing part of the project and normalizes potential bad news. It's like living in a hurricane-prone area where you always need to have emergency supplies and know your evacuation route. You don't know if or when a hurricane may occur, but you're prepared for it to happen.

Individual project risk is an uncertain event or condition, that if it occurs, has a positive or negative effect on one or more project objectives.[8]

–PMBOK Guide

The concept of risk is another theory that I appreciate about project management because it allows for conversations about difficult topics in a neutral way. No project manager wants to talk about their budget getting cut just like no parent wants to talk about their salary getting cut. But if you think about it in advance and have some coping strategies in place, you'll be more clear-headed and faster to address it when it happens. Considering risks in advance prepares us for what life throws at us—for example, having a backup childcare plan already in place so that you don't have to miss work if your normal caregiver calls out sick. This preparation reduces our stress levels, makes our kids feel secure, and helps us resolve issues quickly.

Here, we'll consider our project to be managing our family and risks to be anything that can impact the priorities that we identified with the stop sign in Chapter 3: budget, parents' work, kids' education, family-related work, extracurricular activities and hobbies, health and safety, and quality of life. As you read through this chapter, think of things that keep you up at night and otherwise cause you to worry. As we work through the chapter, you can decide how probable those things are, what their impact would be, and how they should be addressed. We'll look at examples of risks for a family in three common categories, as well as how to manage risks with teenagers. You'll find a risk management plan template at the end of the chapter that you can fill in.

Risk Management Planning

Let's start our risk management planning by classifying risks into three main categories: schedule, budget, and performance.

- **Schedule**—items that impact the family calendar or deadlines. These may include last-minute requests from work or a caregiver who's running late.
- **Budget**—items that affect the family financial plan, like an unexpected expense. This could be a house or car repair, or even a financial gift that has a positive effect on the budget.
- **Performance**—items that impact family quality of life, health and safety, and school and work performance. Examples may include a serious illness or poor school grades.

These three categories capture the most important risks for families. For parents, the family schedule can be stressful because it is often hectic and seems to have almost no leeway. If something pops up unexpectedly on the calendar, it can cause a lot of anxiety. Items that impact the family budget and performance should be closely monitored to protect financial health, quality of life, and work/school.

These risks are interconnected and can affect each other. Running late for childcare pickup can impact the budget if you have to pay late fees. Unplanned costs like a car repair can impact quality of life by adding more stress. Being prepared for these risks and resolving them quickly provides peace of mind and protects what is important to the family.

Below, we'll develop a risk management plan. This involves:

1. Identifying Specific Risks
2. Evaluating Risks
3. Developing Responses
4. Implementing Risk Responses
5. Monitoring your Risk Management Plan

Identifying Specific Risks

To identify risks, start with a brainstorming session. You may want to leave the kids out of this to avoid worrying them unnecessarily with hypothetical risks. During your brainstorming session, have one person write down the ideas from each of the three categories. To get the conversation started, you can ask questions like: What could go wrong with our schedule or budget? What could negatively impact our family's quality of life, our work, our kids' education, or our health and safety? What if...?

Keep in mind that people in your family will probably have different levels of risk tolerance. What seems like a major risk to you might not seem that way to your partner. You can determine which risks you want to address in the following evaluation stage. Give yourself some time to think about it and come back to revise the list.

As a starting point, let's think through a list of possible risks for a family within the three categories:

Schedule:

- Caregiver calls in sick on workday
- Business trip comes up
- Parent running late for childcare pickup

Budget:

- Unexpected car repair is needed
- Spouse is laid off from work
- Large house repair needed

Performance:

- Kids' grades aren't meeting expectations
- Teenager caught drinking alcohol
- Parents feel disconnected from each other

Another way to think through potential risks is to consider each individual separately. Think about each child and their unique situation and whether there's anything to be prepared for. In my family, because of my son's food allergies, a risk would be him having an anaphylactic reaction away from home. Another risk we've thought about is how to get home from our offices near Washington,

DC if there's a terrorist attack. If you live in an area that's prone to natural disasters, what would you do? Because this could easily turn into an anxiety-producing exercise of potential bad news, evaluate and focus on the risks you should be most concerned about next.

Evaluating Risks

To decide which risks to address, evaluate them to see which ones are the most relevant to your family. Do this by determining each risk's level of impact and likelihood of occurrence.

- **Impact**—the strength or magnitude of effect
- **Likelihood**—the probability of it happening

Impact is the strength of effect on something; for example, a high-impact risk would have a high positive or negative effect on your family's priorities, like quality of life, budget, etc. Likelihood is the chance of a risk occurring.

Classify the impact and likelihood of various risks as high, medium, or low. To start the conversation, you can ask these questions: What is the impact of this risk to our family—high, medium, or low? What is the probability of this risk occurring—high, medium, or low?

Then, focus first on the risks that are most likely and have the highest potential impact. Ask yourself: What risks are urgent and must be addressed now? Low-impact and low-likelihood risks are the least important items. For example, planning what to do if an asteroid strikes your area is probably not worth your time, whereas planning for your kids being home from school on a snow day probably is. Evaluate the risks to determine which ones matter the most. You may find some urgent risks that require immediate attention, in which case you would want to move straight to developing risk responses.

Developing Risk Responses

Now that the risk evaluation process has shown you which ones to focus on, you can come up with a risk response. A risk response is your plan to address or resolve risks should they happen. Your response should be in accordance with the level of potential impact; larger impacts will require a larger response, while smaller impacts will require a smaller one. There's no need to overengineer the response for each risk.

Risk responses are worth a lengthy conversation with your partner to find solutions you can agree on. To discuss and determine planned risk responses, ask the following questions: What can we do about it? What is the best way to address it? There could be several different options to consider for each risk. For example, are you comfortable with a neighbor providing backup childcare, or would you prefer a childcare facility? Talk it through until you have a plan that you're both comfortable with, knowing that the plan can be updated and tweaked in the future.

To manage the risk of my son having an allergic reaction to shellfish, he has an EpiPen. We also inform his school and caregivers about his potential need for the medication. For a terrorist attack on Washington, DC, we developed a plan for how to get home if we were working downtown.

We want to be prepared for the threats (negative risks) as well as the opportunities (positive risks) to our family. For example, what if a large work bonus came through? Would you buy something you have always wanted or save the money? Because finances often cause conflict with couples, it is well worth a conversation to understand in advance what you plan to do.

Once you know what your response will be, get ready for it. For example, it may take time to interview and check references for backup babysitters or visit childcare facilities. A plan isn't helpful unless it's ready to be implemented, so discuss who's responsible for each related task. If you're prepared in advance, you'll be able to sleep better at night and be ready to put your plan into action.

A particular response can address more than one risk. For example, finding backup childcare can address several risks to the family schedule. Here's an example of a family risk management plan where several of the risks have the same response.

Family Risk Management Plan

Risk	Impact	Likelihood	Response Plan
Schedule Risks			
Childcare not available one day	High	Medium	Find backup babysitter (relative, alternate childcare center).
Snow day on school day	High	Low	Find backup babysitter/childcare.

Unexpected business trip	Medium	Medium	Grandparents take kids to school.
Late from work to pick up child from daycare	Medium	Medium	Ask neighbor to be backups for each other.
Bad traffic and little time to cook dinner	Medium	High	Stock backup dinners in freezer. Have sandwiches or snacks, stock angel hair pasta and tomato sauce in pantry for quick dinner.
Budget Risks			
Job loss	High	Low	Save 3 months of living expenses.
House/car repairs needed	Medium	Medium	Build up savings plan.
Job raise or financial gift	Medium	Medium	Build up savings plan.
Serious health issue or emergency	High	Medium	Health insurance coverage.
Performance Risks			
Poor school grades	Medium	Medium	Check homework assignments daily, teacher conferences.
Teenager caught drinking alcohol	Medium	Medium	Discuss alcohol usage with them as a pre-teen. Restricted privileges if occurs.
Teenager uses car without permission	Medium	Medium	Inform them when they get driver's license of expectations and responsibilities. Loss of car privileges for two weeks.
Parents feel disconnected from each other	High	High	Monthly date nights and use backup babysitter.
Natural disaster/national emergency	High	Low	Stock emergency supplies and create evacuation plan.

Implementing Risk Responses

Implementing risk responses means putting your plan into action. If something happens, follow your plan, and then evaluate if the response was adequate. Check back with your kids and partner on how it went and see if they have any suggestions. If you need to make some changes to the response plan, make updates to the plan and complete any prework as necessary so you're ready the next time. For example, if you had an expensive car repair come up and there wasn't enough money in the emergency fund, increase your monthly savings to be ready for the next unexpected expense.

Monitoring Risks

Once you have your risk response plan written down, make a note to revisit it once or twice a year, especially if it's outdated or you've found a better solution. In our case, we need to remember to refill my son's EpiPen prescription every year and update our emergency travel plan when our commute changes. This is also a good time to think through whether any new risks have developed or previously identified risks are no longer relevant. As our children get older, the risks we have as a family will change as well. It may warrant another brainstorming session with your partner to think through how family risks have evolved.

I've had to readdress childcare coverage risks in several different phases of my child's development. When he was a baby, we had three different providers who cared for him on different days. This worked well for backup childcare coverage because if one person was unavailable, one of the other two probably were. It was also handy for babysitting, and thus my husband and I were able to have regular date nights. That worked for a few years until the caregivers were no longer available. After that, we tried a few different childcare facilities, eventually finding one we were all happy with. Monitor and adjust the risk management plan as needed to meet your family's priorities.

Managing Risky Teenage Behavior

Talking to your kids about risks as they grow into teenagers can facilitate conversations to better prepare them for future situations. By giving them the opportunity to think about the consequences of their actions beforehand, you can lay the groundwork for them to make wise decisions. This can be a terrific opportunity to have a conversation about difficult subjects in a neutral way. You can discuss them calmly and rationally without the range of emotions that may occur during a difficult situation. They may also open up about the challenges they are facing in school and other areas.

To get the conversation started, ask them questions like: What could negatively impact your school grades, sports performance, or college prospects? What if one of your friends asks you to do something harmful or illegal? What if you make a bad choice and don't know what to do about it? What would you do if you were at a party and someone offered you drugs? If you're out with the car and get drunk, how will you get home?

Once you've spent some time talking about risks, brainstorm potential solutions together. To help them develop their critical thinking skills, ask for their ideas first and then talk through it. That way they're identifying their own principles, not just following yours, and you can guide them if you think they aren't taking something seriously enough or don't understand the possible ramifications. You could also inform them of the consequences from your perspective, like what privileges they might lose at home.

Having these conversations with your teenager before a difficult situation arises helps improve communication, identify positive solutions, and equip them to make more informed decisions. It also leaves the door open to talk about nuances of different situations after they occur, instead of shutting the conversation down. For example, they may say, "I knew it was wrong to ride with someone who was drunk, but I wasn't sure what to do because they were my ride home.' You can then continue to talk through an alternate solution so they can continue to learn and make a wiser choice the next time. In the future, they will be more likely to come talk to you when something happens, since you've been considering difficult situations together, and they will know that you have their best interests at heart.

Example: Family Risk Management Plan

A couple with toddlers and teenagers wants to assess the risks to their family and feel more prepared for surprises. The parents sit down together and discuss what can go wrong and what can negatively impact their family's quality of life. They input the answers in the first column of the risk response plan chart. Conversations revolve around budget, schedule, and performance risks that would impact the family priorities of parents' work, kids' education, family-related work, extracurricular activities and hobbies, health and safety, and quality of life.

Then the parents rank the level of impact and likelihood of each risk as high, medium, or low. After that, they prepare a response plan for the top risks by asking: What can we do about it and what is the best way to address it? The parents then take steps to ensure that the plan could be activated, like asking a grandma to be a backup babysitter and starting an emergency savings account.

When a snow day occurs, they implement their backup childcare plan. Unfortunately, Grandma isn't available, and one of the parents must take a day off from work. Later, they decide to change their backup childcare plan to a daycare facility with drop-off options. Mom agrees to sign the necessary paperwork with the childcare facility so they will be ready for the next snow day. They schedule time on the family calendar to review the risk management plan in six months.

Finding ways to prepare for unexpected surprises protects what is important to your family. It may take some work, but the peace of mind is worth the effort.

Exercises

Exercise #1: Family Risk Management Plan Creation

A. Discuss the following questions with your partner in relation to your family categories of schedule, budget, and performance. Write potential risks in the chart below.
   i.   What can go wrong?
   ii. What could negatively impact our family's quality of life, budget, parents' work, kids' education, family-related work, extracurricular activities and hobbies, and health and safety?
   iii. What if…?
B. Rank level of impact and likelihood of occurrence as high, medium, or low for each risk.
   i.   What is the impact of this risk to our family: high, medium, or low?
   ii. What is the probability of this risk occurring: high, medium, or low?
C. Discuss and determine planned risk responses for each one.
   i.   What can we do about it?
   ii. What is the best way to address it?
D. Implement risk management plan for top risks.
   i.   What risks are urgent and have to be addressed now?
   ii. What risks are high impact and high likelihood?
E. Schedule time on the calendar to revisit the family risk management plan in one year.

Exercise #2: Teenager Risk Management Discussion

A. Discuss risks with your teenager and generate responses with them.
   i.   What could negatively impact your school grades / sports performance / college prospects?
   ii. What if one of your friends asks you to do something harmful or illegal?
   iii. What if you make a bad choice and don't know what to do about it?
   iv. What is the best way to address it? And what can we do about it?

Risk Management Plan

Risk	Impact (H, M, L)	Likelihood (H, M, L)	Risk Response

Step 3

SUCCEED AS A FAMILY

Chapter 10
Being Agile:
Focusing on What's Most Important

TOP TIPS FOR CREATING AN AGILE ENVIRONMENT:

· ·

1. Focus on the satisfaction of the entire family and set goals together.

2. Empower the kids to learn to do the work.

3. Keep it simple and celebrate successes along the way.

· ·

Congratulations! You've learned the techniques that professional project managers apply to million-dollar business initiatives. The goal of this book isn't to create more paperwork; it's to help you achieve the results you want in school performance, family dynamics, work productivity, and other areas of your life, and have fun in the process. Now we're going to look at how you can customize your techniques and way of working to benefit your family and growing children. This is the third step of our Project Management for Parents framework—to succeed as a family.

In this chapter, we'll talk about what it means to have an "Agile mindset" and how focusing on people rather than processes is the key to success. This may seem counterintuitive coming from a project manager, but we use Agile methods as a hybrid approach in the corporate world. The Agile approach is a business perspective that can help you create a high-performing team at home. It's especially relevant to older children because it fosters skill development and independence. It also focuses on achieving desired results for the entire family rather than wasting time on needless processes and paperwork. Here we'll talk through the values that embody the Agile viewpoint. In the next chapter, you'll learn how to select the right tools and techniques for each project or phase in your parenting journey.

The Agile perspective was created by software engineers who were frustrated by the failure rate of projects due to inflexibility and lack of customer input. Traditional projects were defined early and then didn't change much, if at all, until they were launched several years later. Often, by that point, the product was outdated or another company had launched a similar product. These engineers came up with new recommendations, known as The Agile Manifesto, which were incorporated into software design and other types of projects. Applying these principles resulted in faster product delivery and increased customer and project team satisfaction. I've adapted the Agile principles to families and projects at home. These modified principles are:

- Communicate and collaborate.
- Empower your people.
- Deliver simple excellence.
- Learn and change.
- Celebrate!

First, consider the diagram below. Notice that your main goal is family satisfaction. The surrounding circles, which describe unique ways to work as a team, support this main goal. We'll look at these values, and how they relate to family life, next.

The Main Goal: Family Satisfaction

The first premise of Agile management is that individuals are more important than processes—that is, people are more important than any project. The Agile perspective focuses on the customer first, not a checklist of bureaucratic processes that must be followed. In our case, the "customer" is our family, which includes the parents. We want to be aware of everyone's needs because our success is based on meeting them to the greatest extent possible. Because family satisfaction is our main goal, we should focus on that goal and how each project can support it. Each family member's desires may be different, but we can consider all of their opinions to get as close as possible to the optimal outcome. In business, this is called being "customer-centric." Here, we can call it being "family-centric."

Our highest priority is to satisfy the customer.[9]

–Agile Alliance

That's why it's important to keep the family involved throughout a project and ensure that what is being accomplished is what they want or need. Get their input early and check back often to make sure everyone is still on board. For example, if you spend weeks planning a vacation to the mountains without involving your family and only later find out that they all want to go to the beach instead, your efforts will have been wasted.

Now that we've established our main goal of family satisfaction, let's talk about how the other five aspects of the Agile principles can support that goal.

Communicate and Collaborate

If the highest priority is to satisfy the family, we should get their input by communicating and collaborating with them regularly. This can be achieved by frequent, face-to-face, cooperative conversation.

The Agile principles recommend that teams communicate daily, and I think this is a good recommendation for families as well. Discussing items often ensures better understanding and catches problems and misunderstandings early. You can address and resolve issues quickly before they get out of hand. For example, regularly discussing how school is going with your kids can prevent surprises when grades come out at the end of the semester. Have a short family meeting to discuss what's going well, what's not going so well, what people may need help with, and what they're going to focus on next. This can be done any time, such as during a meal or while in the car. Remember that even older kids will appreciate the interest and support, even though they may not show it, because you're keeping the door open for them to communicate with you.

Agile principles specifically identify face-to-face conversations as the most effective means of communication. A lot of meaning can be lost and misunderstandings can happen through text and email or over the phone, so speak in person whenever possible. As our kids get older and are doing things more independently and online, we should make time to sit down and talk to them personally.

Collaboration is a great skill for our kids to learn. It teaches them how to speak up for their ideas, persuade others to see the benefits of their ideas, and consider other people's opinions. "Create psychological safety" is one of the guidelines from the Disciplined Agile mindset, which evolved from the original principles.[10] Creating a nonjudgmental environment is important for the family to want to collaborate, and they will be more apt to share ideas if they know they will be heard. When brainstorming, hold back on critiquing your family's ideas; build on each other's ideas first before narrowing it down to the solution.

Practicing brainstorming and collaboration skills at home will equip your kids for school and, eventually, the workforce. Contributing ideas for a project also enables ownership in the outcome because everyone has had a part in the decision-making. For example, when my son suggested we go camping for Thanksgiving, he reminded us throughout the trip that it was his idea and took great pride in how much we enjoyed it.

Empower Your People

Empowerment is giving someone the authority to do something on their own. And, let's face it, if we don't empower our children, then the work doesn't get done or we have to do it ourselves.

As parents, our ability to empower our kids increases as they get older. Younger kids require more teaching, direction, and training to learn how to do things. This could be toilet training, reading, making their beds, or riding their bikes. As our kids get older, we can pull back and equip them to do homework independently, make dinner, and go out on their own.

When we empower them and step back, kids learn the natural consequences of their actions and can internalize their motivation. For example, if they're late to sports practice and have to run extra laps, they will be motivated to leave on time in the future, without nagging. The idea is to gradually give them space to be more self-sufficient and then support them as necessary.

The teenage years can be a tough time for parents and kids. Kids are trying to figure out who they are while becoming more independent, and parents are trying to keep them safe while learning to loosen the reins and prepare them for adulthood. The Agile mindset can facilitate this process by giving kids the independence they crave in a structured manner that still incorporates the parents' input and family goals. Agile practices embrace self-organized and self-directed teams to create the best results. If you have older children, you can embrace this philosophy and enable them to oversee their own work and decision-making. You can provide more autonomy by creating objectives together but letting them organize and do the work as long as they're following family goals and guidelines.

Empowerment is motivating to our kids as they strive to become their own people. They can take pride in their own work and learn to be independent. Provide children with training and support and then trust them to get the work done. This encourages kids to be more autonomous, which is what we ultimately want for them as adults.

> *Simplicity—the art of maximizing the amount of work not done—is essential.*[11]
>
> *–The Agile Alliance*

Deliver Simple Excellence

As a parent, I really appreciate the Agile focus on keeping it simple. In fact, Agile principles say that simplicity is imperative and recommend putting in the least amount of effort—*not* doing as much work as possible—as long as you achieve the desired result. In other words, what tasks can you avoid while still accomplishing what you want to accomplish? These counterintuitive recommendations put the focus back on delivering family value. In other words, put in the right amount of effort to get the work done well and don't overcomplicate it.

If you focus on simple excellence, your family won't be burdened by the work, and you'll achieve your goal of family satisfaction. Think about how you're getting tasks done. Beware not to overload your family with unnecessary processes or procedures. Don't use a complicated chore chart if it's too time-consuming for the family. Find the smallest amount of process that will support the work, and no more. If you go through this book and something is too complicated, then simplify it, don't use it, or try something else.

Think about your expectations and which ones could be adjusted to avoid overwhelming your family while still achieving what you want. Keeping it simple enables you to make changes more quickly. This ties into the next value: embracing learning and change.

Learn and Change

There's a saying that, in parenting, everything is a phase. Once you get used to one thing about your child, they will grow into another phase. Remembering this enables us to stay flexible as our kids mature, to be adaptable and do what works to support their growth.

Our kids need to learn to adapt as well. Do you want your kids to get frustrated if something isn't perfect at the beginning? Do you want them to get stressed out and anxious if they make a mistake? If not, teach them to try and fail to build resilience, creativity, and grit. When you're trying something new at home, have them suggest a few ways of doing it. Then have them test their own ideas and learn from them. If it's not working, try something else, talk about it, and apply discoveries to the next idea. Keep evolving and trying new things.

One way to continuously improve is to reflect on how a project went with your family. Agile literature calls this a "retrospective," which involves looking back on the project and learning from it. During a family meeting, ask these three questions: What went well? What didn't go so well? What could we learn to do better next time? Once you've identified some problems, brainstorm possible solutions. Try the solution to see if it works. If it does, great! Keep doing it. If that solution doesn't work, try something else. This provides a learning opportunity for all family members, including parents. It can also help foster a better home environment for everyone in the long term and improve family satisfaction and results on the next project.

For example, on the Thanksgiving camping trip, getting my son to pack was a challenge. We learned that asking him in the moment to do certain tasks didn't work. So, we later discussed it with him and decided that next time we would decide over breakfast who wanted to do which tasks to ensure the entire family was clear on expectations. These mini family meetings create a continuous learning cycle, which promotes ongoing communication and improvement.

By embracing learning and change, we teach our kids that their input is valued, and they learn to adopt flexibility and problem-solving. This also creates more openness on their part because they will share with you when something goes wrong. They will be less apt to hide something from you because they know that you'll support them as a person, even in their failures. Supporting their learning process lets them know that you have their back while encouraging them to become more independent, creative, honest, and resilient. These skills will serve them well as they grow into adults.

Create effective environments that foster joy.[12]

–Project Management Institute

Celebrate!

The Disciplined Agile mindset encourages a positive working culture. One of the guidelines is to "create effective environments that foster joy." One way to foster joy within your family is by recognizing them. Kids love to celebrate and feel validated. By clearly communicating what is being celebrated, you'll reinforce the behaviors, and your kids will be more likely to repeat them. Celebrating motivates them and keeps them engaged in what you're working on. The sooner you celebrate a small success, the more interested they will stay in the project. Conversely, if you wait too long to recognize something positive, they may lose enthusiasm.

One way to motivate kids is to let them choose the goal and the reward. Come up with a goal together that can be achieved relatively quickly, like the kids completing all their homework for that week. Then decide on a reward that they're excited about, like extra screen time. When they hit a larger milestone, like achieving a certain grade point average for the school semester, make it a larger celebration, like going out to dinner at their favorite restaurant or a special event with their friends. Give them a goal to reach and then celebrate in a way that they will enjoy.

To recognize your kids, verbal praise is great, but try to think outside the box. For example, get ice cream to celebrate all the chores getting done that week, or go see a movie when a school quarter is completed successfully. Here are a few ideas for celebrating family successes to reinforce desired behaviors:

- Have a special meal together and let the kids pick the menu.
- Do one of their preferred activities together, like going to an amusement park or a play place.
- Bake a cake.
- Buy them a toy.
- Make them a card.
- Give them special privileges, like staying up late or going out with their friends.
- Have a game night.
- Hold a party with balloons and cupcakes.
- See a movie.
- Have a dance party.

In summary, to create a positive, motivating environment, recognize and honor accomplishments, both large and small. Your kids will stay more engaged in the work and be more likely to repeat the behaviors.

Example: Empowering a Teenager with Schoolwork

Empowering a teenager to manage schoolwork independently equips them with skills that will serve them for a lifetime, including in college and in their careers. To empower a teenager with homework, the parent and child should first agree on goals and then implement supporting processes around them.

Say a teenager has been struggling with the first half of middle school, and her grades are lower than expected. Dad has several conversations with her about it, and she tells him that it's been hard to organize her work with different teachers for each class. They both agree that she should get higher grades. Together, they determine specific goals: a 3.0 grade point average, completing 90 percent of her homework, and no more than three absences per semester.

Next, Dad asks her what she needs help with, and she mentions keeping track of her homework. Dad offers her some options, like recording assignments in a notebook, spreadsheet, or app during school. She decides on the notebook to write down assignments and agrees to take the notebook to every class. Then they agree to weekly check-in meetings to see how things are going. They discuss what's going well and not so well, what she needs help with, and what work she has over the next week. Dad agrees to provide support when asked. Once they agree on the process, Dad makes an effort to step back and not overmanage her homework. He waits for the weekly check-in to discuss the schoolwork unless his daughter brings it up before then.

During a check-in meeting, they review mid-semester grades. The teenager is getting a 3.0 in every class except for science. She says the concepts are difficult to understand, and they decide that a study group would be a good idea. She agrees to reach out to some friends in her class the next week to get the group started. At the next weekly meeting, she says the kids aren't available for a study group, so they brainstorm some more ideas. They decide that she will reach out to her teacher to see if there are open office hours for questions. It's difficult for Dad not to intervene more with science class, but he knows that it's more helpful for her to try things on her own.

When the end-of-semester grades come out, her science grade has improved! He makes her favorite dessert for dinner and gives her a card, telling her that he's proud of her for not giving up on science class and for trying different solutions.

The Agile mindset enables us to achieve our goals quickly and efficiently, and parents can be less stressed by keeping things simple. These family-centric principles keep us focused in a collaborative way, creating a stronger team. Applying the Agile values also teaches our kids independence, creativity, flexibility, and problem-solving—all skills that are essential as they transition to adulthood. And if we get to eat a few cupcakes as we celebrate our successes along the way, so much the better!

Exercises

Exercise #1: Selecting and Applying Agile Principles

Discuss this chapter with your partner and decide what goals you want to achieve as a family. Pick the top two Agile principles that you think your family would most benefit from implementing:

1.

2.

Discuss with your family what these two concepts mean and whether they think they would be helpful, how to achieve your goal, and how to implement these principles collaboratively.

Chapter 11
BRINGING IT ALL TOGETHER: TOP TIPS AND REAL-LIFE EXAMPLES

TOP TIPS TO BRING IT ALL TOGETHER:

• •

1. Building teamwork and gaining buy-in is the crucial first step for a productive work environment.

2. Establish your approach by focusing on family priorities and involving them in identifying the work.

3. Succeed by empowering the family and tailoring techniques while having fun.

• •

Y ou've learned the fundamentals of project management and are equipped to organize your family's activities more effectively and efficiently. You're now ready to create a loving, productive environment for your family members, one based on shared objectives, trust, commitment, and accountability!

In this chapter, we'll bring all the content together and summarize the top tips I've shared throughout the book. These principles represent the project life-cycle. I'll used the example of building a treehouse to illustrate how a project moves through the process from beginning to end. Then we'll rightsize all the project tools we've learned and apply them to examples of small, medium, and large projects at home. After reading this chapter, you'll have a ready library of project tools to reference for your next project at home. Use this the next time you're about to start a new project.

Top Tips

As a refresher, let's recap the three *Project Management for Parents* steps and the top tips I've shared. The three steps are (1) build teamwork, (2) establish your approach to getting the work done, and (3) empower each other to succeed as a family. Building teamwork is the crucial first step for a united and productive family work environment—without it, many projects fail. Communication is the foundation to establishing your approach so that everyone is involved and aware of what is expected of them. Your collective goals can be reached more quickly and equitably through empowerment, by equipping the entire family to participate. Below, I recap important tips from each chapter for accomplishing each step.

Step 1: Build Teamwork to take the crucial first step toward a united and productive family work environment. Ensure buy-in among the project leaders first before moving forward with a project. Communicate the benefits and support family members to help them embrace the project.

- Define your family mission and values.
- Build teamwork with family activities.
- Encourage communication and ownership with regular family meetings.
- Ensure parents/project leaders agree on the reasons for and benefits of any project.
- Communicate early and often with your "team" about the project and benefits.

- Support the family members emotionally and functionally throughout the project.

Step 2: Establish Your Approach by focusing on your priorities and involving your family in identifying the work and who will do what. Ensure that everyone is aware of what is expected of them and make the work fun while communicating often and managing risks.

- Determine your family's priorities and rightsize your family plan as needed.
- Involve the family in determining the work to be done.
- Use the simplest documentation process required for each project.
- Have regular meetings to check the status of work.
- Make work fun with games and rewards.
- Develop a management plan for top risks to your family.

Step 3: Succeed as a Family by empowering each other and tailoring these techniques to achieve the results that you want in any area, such as family dynamics, work, or school performance. Use the simplest project management supporting processes that provide value, and make changes as often as needed.

- Focus on the satisfaction of the entire family and set goals.
- Empower the entire family to do work and celebrate accomplishments.
- Experiment and adjust as necessary.
- Rightsize the processes for each project.

Project Management Lifecycle

Collectively, these tips follow the sequence of a project from beginning to end. A project happens over a period of time and includes the same four phases: initiation, planning, execution, and close-out. Before a project is started, the initiation phase determines why the project is being done and defines what you want to achieve. Once the project is approved, more detailed research is completed during the planning phase. Next, the project is created during the execution phase. Finally, in the close-out phase, the work is reviewed and closed out if it was done correctly.

Remember that the initiation phase is the most important because everyone has to agree on the project. If the parents don't agree on the benefits or the budget, then it's better to stop the project in the initiation phase rather than begin something that may not be successful.

1. **Initiation Phase =**
   Generating idea for project and gaining approval

2. **Planning Phase =**
   Obtaining more information and determining what will happen

3. **Execution Phase =**
   Getting the work done to build the project

4. **Close-out Phase =**
   Checking the work and finishing the project

These four phases provide a consistent sequence to reference and follow the same flow as the chapters of this book. Building your team and determining priorities and what you want to do comes first. After you've agreed to move forward, you identify the work, figure out who does what, and get it done while managing risks.

The different tools that we've covered provide the structure to support this project lifecycle. These tools are used at different stages, like the scope document in the initiation phase. Other documents are created in the planning phase and managed during the execution phase, e.g., communications plan, action item list, timeline. These tools provide the information to design, manage, and deploy each project.

Example: Building a Treehouse

Let's illustrate the project management lifecycle and tools at a high level with a family that wants to build a treehouse in their backyard.

Project Initiation

During the project initiation phase, the parents meet initially and discuss the treehouse using the scope document. As leaders with the resources to support the project, they must decide that this is something that they want and can afford to do before the project can proceed. They consider any risks like the strength of the tree and document them in the risk management plan. Tools that can help with this step include:

- Scope Document = Build a fun fort in the large tree in the backyard with two rooms, four windows, roof, door, and rope ladder with a budget of $600 USD.
- Risk management plan = Determine if tree can safely bear weight of fort.

 ## Project Planning

Once the project is approved, it moves on to the planning phase. At that point, the parents discuss it with the kids and ask them what kind of treehouse they would like (features, color, etc.) The parents consider designs and determine the budget. They also consider who should be involved and document it on the communications plan. The final design is approved by the parents and children and tasks are documented on the action item list. Tools for this step include:

- Communications plan = Inform neighbor with adjoining yard of plan and ask uncle to help build it.
- Action Item List = Buy supplies at store, build, paint, and test.

 ## Project Execution

The execution phase is when the actual construction of the treehouse happens; the supplies are purchased, and the treehouse is built and painted. Work is tracked on the timeline and marked complete on the action item list.

- Timeline = Build frame > build walls > build roof > paint > decorate

 ## Project Close-out

In the final phase, the fort is evaluated for safety, and the kids determine if it reaches its goal of being fun! The work area is cleaned up and invoices are paid (hopefully at or under budget). Then the project is considered completed. If you think you'll be doing a similar project in the future, it can be useful to save your project documents and note any lessons learned from the project for future reference.

This is the project lifecycle and supporting tools to use for building a treehouse. However, if you were tackling a bigger building project, like renovating a kitchen, you could consider adding more supporting tools, like check-in meetings. Adjusting the tools you use for a project is called "tailoring," so let's talk about what that looks like.

Tailoring Project Tools

We covered a lot of different techniques in this book, like risk management plans and timelines. However, you don't have to use them all for every project. Rather, depending on the size and complexity of your project at home, you can select which processes to use. Smaller projects may just require an action item list, while larger projects might benefit from all of processes we've discussed. Project management can be as simple or as robust as necessary. When we modify our project management approach based on the size and complexity of each project, project managers call this "tailoring."

Tailoring is necessary because each project is unique; therefore, not every process, input, tool, technique, or output is required on every project.[13]

–PMBOK Guide

The same tailoring approach should be used for our family projects. Parents are very busy and have to keep things simple. The project management processes should provide value to you and be worth the effort. Using the tools we've discussed should make life easier and reduce effort in the long term. With that in mind, let's talk about which tools are most useful for small, medium, and large projects.

 Small Project
- Task List

 Medium Project
- Scope Document
- Task List
- Communication Plan
- Check-In Meetings

 Large Project
- Scope Document
- Task List
- Communication Plan
- Check-In Meetings
- Timeline
- Risk Management Plan

The size of the project dictates the amount of paperwork required to support it and keep it organized. Small projects need less support, while larger, more complex projects require more. Project size is determined by the number of people involved and the amount of money and work required. A small project might be organizing chores, a medium project might be planning an event like a birthday party, and a large project might be moving the family to a new town.

Notice that the project management documents listed for a small or medium project are also included for large projects, so the resource list builds with project size. A small project requires a task list to keep track of what has to be done by whom; tasks can easily be tracked on a simple sheet of paper, whiteboard, or spreadsheet. In addition to a task list, a medium project will benefit from a scope document, to ensure that the leaders agree to the work and understand the project benefits. A medium project will also call for a communications plan to ensure that everyone involved with or affected by the project is aware of what is happening and can support the work. Large projects require more tools to ensure that all the work is completed well and on time.

Depending on what works best for you and your family, you can pick and choose which tools you want to use. Here is a list of additional tools that are available to support different aspects of projects.

- Family Priorities Exercise
- IN/OUT Family Plan List
- Chore Chart
- Kanban Board
- Meeting Minutes
- Family Meeting Agenda

Templates of these tools are included in the subsequent chapter and can also be downloaded from www.projectmanagementforparents.com.

Real-Life Examples

Now that we understand the flow of projects and that each one is different, let's look at specific examples throughout kids' lives and how to apply project management tools in a relevant way. We'll look at projects during kids' life stages and discuss how you can rightsize tools from the book.

Infancy/Toddler:
- **Determining family priorities** sets the stage for satisfaction in the family, knowing you are all working toward the appropriate goals for you. This exercise is especially relevant when kids are infants because this is a

major life change for the parents, and babies require so much care and time. The exercises at the ends of Chapters 3 and 4 enable decision-making on how to spend your time. The IN/OUT of Family Plan exercise outlines the changes that will be made to meet your goals. These tools can clarify what works for your family whenever you feel that something is out of balance or your priorities may need a reset.

> » Family Priorities Exercise
> » IN/OUT Family Plan List

- **Selecting a childcare provider (and backup)** is a small- or medium-sized project (depending on the situation) that will greatly relieve stress when completed! Chapter 9 outlines how to identify gaps in your childcare plan and develop a response to fill them. Use a task list while implementing your risk management plan to keep track of the different steps required, like checking babysitter references or visiting childcare facilities. Here are the recommended tools:

  > » Risk Management Plan
  > » Action Item List
  > » Contact List

- **Meal planning** is an ongoing small project where reference documentation is useful. Chapter 7 covers meal planning and uses a master list of popular dishes to refer to. Analyzing who has the capacity to help with meals and assigning chores can distribute the work more evenly. For large holiday meals, share the work among family members and assign dishes or tasks like setting the table or cleaning the kitchen. For this project, I recommend using:

  > » Master Task List
  > » Optional tools: Weekly Schedule Analysis and Chore Chart

- **Building a treehouse** is a large project that is discussed in Chapter 5 and this chapter. This building project would start with the scope document to clearly outline the work being done and the cost. Once the scope has been outlined, use these project management tools to track the details. These tools can also be used for home renovations.

  > » Scope Document

>> Action Item List
>> Contact List
>> Communications Plan
>> Check-in Meetings
>> Timeline
>> Risk Management Plan

Elementary/High School:
- **Back-to-school planning** is a medium-sized and exciting project for families. Keep in mind the ADKAR Model in Chapter 2 and that your kids may need emotional and functional support with what is a big transition for them. Weekly family meetings can facilitate the conversation about how things are going and how you can support them. These meetings also keep parents informed of any new onboarding items or schedule changes that can be tracked with a task list. Now is a good time to check the weekly schedule and family priorities to ensure that you're not signing up for too many activities. Put new events on the shared calendar and review schedule availability with your partner to attend parent-teacher meetings and back-to-school nights. Recommended tools for this project include:
  >> Action Item List
  >> Contact List
  >> Family Meetings
  >> Weekly Schedule Analysis
  >> Priorities exercise
  >> IN/OUT Family Plan List
  >> Shared Calendar

- **Organizing chores and schoolwork** is a small project using the simplest process possible to keep it manageable. Chapter 7 covers how to identify who does what chores. Chapter 8 covers how to organize schoolwork and chores. Once you have your tracking system set up, a regular family meeting is recommended to review the work. Here are the recommended tools:
  >> Chore Chart, Kanban Board, Weekly Calendar, or Daily Checklist
  >> Family Meeting

- **Birthday party or event planning** is typically a medium-sized project. Chapter 5 starts the project with a scope document. Scoping facilitates an initial discussion with your partner on the size, invitees, location, and cost. Once the event is scoped, a task list keeps track of the work and a communication plan includes regular status meetings and meeting minutes keep track of the details. These tools can be used for planning events like school dances, prom, camping trips, reunions, etc.
  » Scope Document
  » Contact List
  » Communications Plan
  » Meeting Minutes
  » Action Item List
  » Check-in Meetings

- **Summer planning** is a small- to medium-sized project. You'll need to determine activities for the kids while school is out of session. Discussing what kids want to do and determining the budget can be done by reviewing the sections in the scope document as a family. You can also discuss summer vacation preferences and timing. Once you have determined the overall approach, use a task list to manage the various activities like booking summer camps and arranging transportation. Once the plans have been finalized, input them on the shared family calendar to keep track of the schedule. I recommend using:
  » Scope Document
  » Action Item List
  » Contact List
  » Shared Calendar

- **Coordinating schedules** is an ongoing process that's managed with a shared calendar and capacity planning covered in Chapter 7. Once these processes are in place, a family meeting keeps everyone up to date on the latest schedule. Review the family schedule together weekly or daily and talk through any conflicts or changes that need to be addressed. Take advantage of these tools:
  » Resource Capacity Planning
  » Shared Calendar

- **Managing risky teenage behavior** is a difficult project but necessary to address to keep kids safe and healthy. Chapter 9 outlines how to have a conversation with your teen about potentially dangerous situations, how to address them, and the consequences of making poor choices. I recommend starting this project early by having conversations with your pre-teen so they're equipped when the time comes. For this project, you probably only need:
  » Risk Management Plan

- **Empowering a teenager to do schoolwork** is a challenging project but one that will equip them to be successful as an adult. Applying the concept of empowerment discussed in Chapter 10 will provide the hands-off perspective and revisiting the ADKAR Model in Chapter 2 can illustrate where they require support. The first step is to set agreed-upon goals with your child, who can use the weekly schedule analysis or priorities exercise to think through how their time is being used. Once goals have been set for school, activities, etc., this is their opportunity to become their own self-organized team. They can choose what tools they want to use to stay on track. Chapter 8 provides an overview of how to equip them to organize their schoolwork. Once they have established their approach to manage the work, schedule regular check-in meetings to see how it is going and support them as needed. Here is a list of tools to choose from:
  » Weekly Schedule Analysis
  » Priorities Exercise
  » Notebook or daily planner to collect homework assignments
  » Daily checklist (spreadsheet, paper, or app), weekly calendar, or Kanban board
  » Regularly scheduled check-in meetings

- **Applying to college** is a large project that involves a lot of work and people and has a high potential cost and risk. Therefore, the full suite of project management tools is recommended to ensure it has the necessary support. An example of a Work Breakdown Structure for a college application process and timeline is included in Chapter 6. As your child learns about each college, have him take notes on its characteristics (size, programs, etc.) so that he can compare notes later when he is narrowing down the list of schools. This could be done in a spreadsheet with a different tab for each school. Also record impressions after visiting each campus. Here are the tools to support the college application process:

» Scope Document
» Contact List
» Communications Plan
» Action Item List
» Work Breakdown Structure
» Check-in Meetings
» Timeline
» Risk Management Plan

All Ages:

• **Holiday planning** is a small- to medium-sized project that's outlined in Chapter 8. First, hold a brainstorming session with the entire family and discuss the work to be done to prepare for the holidays. Also ask them what fun events they want to include. Then document all the tasks that are involved and assign a person to them on a task list or Kanban Board posted in a visible location. A scope document is optional for parents to outline what the budget is, who is participating, and what they want to happen during this time. Check-in meetings can be done over meals to review the task list and check status of work. Useful tools for this project include:

» Family Meeting
» Action Item List or Kanban Board
» Optional Tools: Scope Document and Check-in Meetings

• **Planning family vacations** is a medium-sized project that requires planning tools and good communication to ensure success. Chapter 5 discusses how to get everyone on the same page so they can be comfortable with the overall plan and enjoy the trip. Because vacation planning can be complicated, a task list keeps track of the work. Regular status meetings can keep planning on track and the family involved in decisions. Here are the recommended tools for planning a family vacation:

» Scope Document

- » Action Item List
- » Contact List
- » Check-in Meetings

- **Changing schools** is a medium-sized project that's discussed in Chapter 2, where the engagement and ADKAR Model sections outline how to support your child during this transition. A task list keeps track of the items to be accomplished and the communications plan and contact list ensures relevant people are kept informed. Weekly family meetings can facilitate the conversation about how things are going and how you can support them during the transition. Consider using a:
  - » Communications Plan
  - » Contact List
  - » Action Item List
  - » Check-in Meetings

- **Moving the family** is a large project that requires significant support. Chapter 2 discusses this project in detail, and I especially recommend reviewing the engagement and ADKAR Model sections that outline how to support family members emotionally. Once the communication plan has been outlined, use the full suite of project management tools to support a very challenging project. These include, among others:
  - » Scope Document
  - » Contact List
  - » Communications Plan
  - » Action Item List
  - » Check-in Meetings
  - » Timeline
  - » Risk Management Plan

- **Managing health issues** is a large, potentially difficult project that often requires the full suite of project management tools to support the family. These tools will assist you in remembering what needs to happen when you may be too stressed to think clearly. Chapter 6 provides examples of preparing for surgery and managing caregivers, and you can also apply these tools to support you through it:

> » Scope Document
> » Contact List
> » Communications Plan
> » Action Item List
> » Check-in meetings with meeting minutes
> » Timeline
> » Risk Management Plan

- **Caring for elderly parents** is an extra-large project that can take years. Since many of us in the sandwich generation will have to address this at some point in our lives, here are some recommendations based on my experience. Resource capacity planning and family priorities are especially important to address early on in this project. The amount of work can be overwhelming, and it is important to share or outsource the work as much as possible. This is a project where quality of life needs to be monitored for the caregiver(s) and the parent(s). I would suggest regularly reviewing priorities and constraints to prevent burnout. The risk management plan enables an honest conversation with siblings and your parents about what is happening. A risk review enables a more neutral conversation with your parents about giving up driving or living alone. This project is often shared among siblings, so a task management app or cloud-based documents can more easily track work and communication. As additional resources, a daily care plan discussed in Chapter 7 and a medication chart are also available in the tools and templates chapter.
  - » Constraints/Priorities Exercise
  - » Resource Capacity Planning
  - » Scope Document
  - » Meeting Minutes
  - » Contact List
  - » Communications Plan
  - » Action Item List / App
  - » Check-in Meetings
  - » Timeline
  - » Risk Management Plan
  - » Daily Care Plan

These examples can also be used as reference for similar projects you want to complete at home. You can pick and choose from the list of tools, and please use the tools that work for you and that you find most useful. Remember that the project management processes should provide value to you and your family and reduce overall workload in the long run by helping you be more organized.

Project management is a powerful framework that has been used by companies for decades to create and deploy new products and services. The beauty of project management is that the same framework applies to different types of projects, and the processes are repeatable. Now that you've read this book, you can reuse the techniques you've learned multiple times for different household responsibilities and even apply them at work too!

I hope the three steps we discussed to build teamwork, establish your approach, and succeed as a family enable you to spend more time on what matters most: each other. Thank you for the opportunity to share these ideas with you. I wish you and your family all the best as you succeed together.

Chapter 12
RESOURCES: TOOLS AND TEMPLATES

TOP TIPS FOR USING PROJECT MANAGEMENT TOOLS:

1. Use the least amount of paperwork necessary to stay organized.

2. Use processes that provide value for the entire family, including the parents.

3. Save completed documents for future reference if a similar project will likely recur.

This chapter provides the project management templates from the book for reference and ease of use. The beauty of project management is that it's a repeatable framework, meaning you can use these same tools over and over again. For example, once you fill in and manage a few action item lists, you'll get better at developing them. Please remember to select processes that provide value and are worth the effort. Regardless of the size of the project, I recommend using the simplest amount of documentation that will still help you achieve your goals.

You can also apply the project management concepts you've learned without necessarily using the paperwork. For example, you may not need to fill out an entire scope document and could merely discuss the different components with your family. Or you could take meeting minutes and note action items but just discuss them and not distribute them via email. I've also had people thank me for providing the meeting minutes and task lists so they didn't have to remember the information. The goal here is family satisfaction and reaching your goals, so modify your approach based on your needs.

These templates can be adapted to any size or type of project. If you find yourself completing a project that's likely to recur, like another child applying to college, hold on to the documents you create so you'll have less work to do the next time.

The tools are listed in the order they appear in the book, which follows the project management lifecycle. There are two additional tools for health issues, like caring for elderly parents, at the end of the chapter. You can also download the documents from www.projectmanagementforparents.com. Good luck!

Family Charter

The _____ Family is _____,
_____, and _____.

1. We'll create an environment of _____, _____,
   and _____.

2. We'll _____, _____, and
   _____.

3. When there's a conflict, we'll _____, _____,
   and _____.

Family Meeting Agenda

1. What worked well this week? Where do we have fully bloomed roses?

2. What did not work well this week? Where did we find thorns?

3. What will we work on next week? Where do we see flower buds?

Family Support Team List

Support Team Member	Level of Impact (1 [low]–5 [high])	Notes

Contact List

Name	Title	Company	Email	Phone

Communications Plan

Communications Plan, Project _____					
To Whom	What	When	How	By Whom	Status

Current Family Plan Analysis

FAMILY CONSTRAINT	CURRENT SITUATION	WEIGHT (#1-4)
Parents' Work		
Kids' Education		
Family-related work		
Activities & Hobbies		
Health & Safety		
Quality of Life		
Total Weight, Current Family Circle		

Total Current Family Circle Size = ____ /24 _____

The total weight shows the size of your family circle:

- 19–24 = large circle; maxing out
- 13–18 = moderate circle; manageable with some white space
- 7–12 = small circle; manageable with much white space
- 0–6 = tiny circle; with need for more to be done

Desired Family Plan Analysis

CONSTRAINT	DESIRED SITUATION	WEIGHT (#1–4)
Parents' Work		
Kids' Education		
Family-related work		
Activities & Hobbies		
Health & Safety		
Quality of Life		
Total Weight, Desired Family Circle		

Total Current Family Circle Size = ___ */24* _____

The total weight shows the size of your family circle:
- 19–24 = large circle; maxing out
- 13–18 = moderate circle; manageable with some white space
- 7–12 = small circle; manageable with much white space
- 0–6 = tiny circle; with need for more to be done

Adjustments to Achieve the Desired Family Plan

Now that you have adjusted your constraints, write out specifically what has changed to rightsize your family plan—what is IN your family plan and what is now OUT of your family plan, e.g., more resources to help like grandparents or fewer kids activities.

In Family Plan:

-
-
-
-
-

Out of Family Plan:

-
-
-
-
-

Scope Document

Project Name:	Date:
Why/Rationale/Success Metrics	What if/Risks
What/Design & Deliverables	Who/People Involved
How/Budget	When/Timing

Meeting Minutes

1. Items discussed

2. Next steps/follow-ups with the people responsible for each item

NEXT STEP/TASK	OWNER NAME

Action Item List

STATUS	TASK	CATEGORY	OWNER	DUE DATE	Notes:

Work Breakdown Structure & Timeline

Pre-Event
•
•
•
•
•
•

Event
•
•
•
•
•
•

Post-Event
•
•
•
•
•
•

Timeline

Weekly Schedule Analysis

Hours/Day	Mon	Tue	Wed	Thu	Fri	Sat	Sun
Sleep							
Prep AM & PM (Dress/Eat)							
Work/School + Commute							
Extracurricular Activities							
Homework							
Exercise							
Chores							
Meal Prep							
Dishes							
Family/Friends							
Total Hours							

Chore Chart

NAME	Daily	Mon	Tue	Wed	Thu	Fri	Sat	Sun

Task Management System—Daily Checklist

Day
-
-
To Do This Week
-
-

Task Management System—Weekly Calendar

Monday	Tuesday	Wednesday	Thursday	Friday	Saturday
-	-	-	-	-	-
-	-	-	-	-	-
-	-	-	-	-	-
-	-	-	-	-	-

Task Management System—Kanban Board

NAME	TO DO	HELP	DOING	DONE
Parking Lot:				

Risk Management Plan

Risk	Impact (H, M, L)	Likelihood (H, M, L)	Risk Response

Additional Tools—Health Projects

Medication List

Week of:

PLEASE INITIAL WHEN COMPLETE

	Sun	Mon	Tue	Wed	Thu	Fri	Sat	Medications
7:00 AM								
11:00 AM								
3:00 PM								
7:00 PM								

Daily Care Plan Example for Caregivers

Morning (7:00 a.m.–3:00 p.m.)

- 7:00 a.m. medication—sign record sheet on dining room table.
- Assist with getting dressed, washing face, and brushing teeth and hair.
- Assist with breakfast.
- 11:00 a.m. medication—sign record sheet on dining room table.
- Assist with lunch.
- Clean up kitchen.
- Assist with taking a shower and washing hair, as needed.
- Assist with ordering dinner and/or note needed groceries on market list on fridge.

Afternoon (3:00 p.m.–11:00 p.m.)

- 3:00 p.m. medication—sign record sheet on dining room table.
- Provide water and remind to drink regularly.
- Clean bathroom.
- With rollator, assist with walking practice up and down hallway.
- Take for walk outside.
- Assist with dinner.
- 7:00 p.m. medication—sign record sheet on dining room table.
- Assist with dressing for bed, washing face, and brushing teeth and hair.
- Assist with getting into bed.

Evening (11:00 p.m.–7:00 a.m.)

- Assist as needed.

Next Steps

As a project manager, you know I couldn't end a book without a call to action! Take a minute and jot down any items from the book that you found particularly helpful; revisiting the top tips summary in Chapter 11 can refresh your memory. Compile the tasks in one place and give yourself a realistic deadline. You can then take that first step in your *Project Management for Parents* journey and manage your work to successful completion.

If you'd like more help along the way, please visit my website: www.project-managementforparents.com. You'll find a download library with the tools and templates found in Chapter 12 in a larger format so you can print them and use them for a variety of projects at home. Additionally, there are videos, articles, and more resources for you to choose from. If you have a moment, please post an online review of *Project Management for Parents* so that more people can hear about it. You can also join my email community from the website to receive ongoing tips and updates.

Thank you for exploring *Project Management for Parents* with me. I hope you experience the power of project management at home.

Acknowledgments

T hey say it takes a village to raise a child, and I think the same is true for writing a book. I could not have done it without the encouragement, feedback, and support of so many people. First and foremost, my husband, Jeff, who happens to be a professional editor; it was fun to work together in a way that we hadn't before in our marriage. I love to see your talents in action and how gifted you are in knowing what I want to write but editing it to be even clearer and more concise. Also, my dear son, without whom this book would not exist; I am so privileged to be your mother, and you bring joy to me every day.

Project Management for Parents would also not be possible without the unwavering support of my previous bosses, Hervé Humler and Kevin Walsh, who enabled me to continue working in project management when I became a parent. I am forever grateful for being able to spend time with my son when he was young while still pursuing my career. Thank you as well to Marla Del Rosario and Cecile Galvin, who were partners in and outside the office, and to Len Wolin, who encouraged my growth as a project manager at the beginning of my career and continues to do so years later.

So many people guided me along the way when *Project Management for Parents* was just an idea in my head. In particular, Judy Umlas of the International Institute for Learning encouraged me to start to write and see if the concept made sense as a book. Your kind nudging kept me moving forward and opened so many doors through an invitation to present at International Project Management Day. Thanks, as well, to Michael Ebeling of Ebeling & Associates for believing in my idea and sharing it with Morgan James Publishing; this book would not have happened so quickly without your generosity. I'm also grateful to David Hancock and the team at Morgan James for investing in me as an author, as well as my editors, Jacqueline Hritz and Aubrey Kosa, for clearly stating what I wanted to say and providing a realistic reader's perspective.

Additional thanks go to all those who provided input and encouragement and made this book better and easier through their efforts:

- My mom and siblings, Alison, Lorraine, and Doug, who cheered me on during our family Zoom calls and provided insights on the book's cover, my website, and my social media approach. And for Lorraine ensuring that teenagers were well represented in the book—thanks for keeping it real.

- Dave of MightyPixel and his wife Catherine—first for your friendship, and then for your honest video and editing feedback.

- Mary Sue for being my trustworthy chapter reviewer and cheerleader. I appreciate your friendship and the time you took on this project.

- Diana for helping me think through the more complicated concepts; it's always good ideating with you.

- Loretta for providing insights when you are so busy creating excellence at school.

- Chelsea for providing feedback as a new parent. I'm so proud of you!

- Colleagues like Bart, author of *Most People Don't (and Why You Should)*, who guided me on this venture and cheered me on along the way. Thanks for doing that!

- Friends who shared texts, prayers, and words of encouragement; you keep me smiling.

- My LinkedIn community, where it all started as an article, was also a big part of this—thank you for the likes and comments along the way.

All this would not be possible without the awesome timing, grace, and favor of my Lord and Savior Jesus Christ. Thank you for using so many of my personal and professional experiences for this book. May I honor You with the work.

Thank you all for this opportunity.

About the Author

Hilary Kinney is the proud mother of an elementary school student and works with companies to achieve their visions through strategic communications and project management. She has 17 years of experience successfully advancing business priorities and deploying major projects for large corporations. Her achievements range from facilitating a C-suite-sponsored customer recognition program across 7,000 properties globally to directing special projects from the president's office at The Ritz-Carlton Hotel Company.

While working at The Ritz-Carlton Corporate Headquarters, she developed global communications to reinforce the company's vision and key success factors and was a founding member of the Corporate Program Management Office. Hilary was proud to be part of the team when The Ritz-Carlton achieved the top-ranked position in the J.D. Power Luxury Hotel Guest Satisfaction Award for seven out of eight years.

Hilary earned a B.S. in Hotel Administration from Cornell University. She holds a Project Management Professional (PMP)˚ Certification from the Project Management Institute, as well as a Change Practitioner Certification from the Prosci˚ Change Management Leadership Center. Hilary lives in the Washington, DC area, where she enjoys outdoor activities with her family.

Endnotes

1. Hilary Kinney, "Project Management for Parents," *IIL Blog*, September 4, 2020. Project Management Update awarded the post one of its 2020 Most Valuable Post Awards (3rd Place, Category: Other).

2. Bruce Feiler, *The Secrets of Happy Families: Improve your Mornings, Tell your Family History, Fight Smarter, Go Out and Play,* and Much More (New York: William Morrow, 2013).

3. ADKAR is a registered trademark of Prosci, inc. Used with permission.

4. Jeffrey M. Hiatt, ADKAR: A Model for Change in Business, Government and Our Community (Loveland, CO: Prosci Research, 2006).

5. Project Management Institute, *PMBOK Guide*, Sixth Edition (Newtown Square, PA: Project Management Institute, 2017), 701.

6. Rachel Pelta, "FlexJobs Survey Shows Need for Flexibility, Support for Working Parents," Job Search Articles, FlexJobs, September 15, 2020.

7. Claire Ewing-Nelson, "Four Times More Women Than Men Dropped Out of the Labor Force in September," National Women's Law Center, October 2, 2020; US Bureau of Labor Statistics, "Table B-1: Employees on Nonfarm Payrolls by Industry Sector and Selected Industry Detail," Economic News Release, accessed March 2, 2021.

8. Project Management Institute, *PMBOK Guide*, 397.

9. "Principles Behind the Agile Manifesto," The Agile Alliance, accessed March 2, 2021.

10. "The Disciplined Agile Foundation Layer," Project Management Institute, accessed March 2, 2021.

11. The Agile Alliance, "Principles Behind the Agile Manifesto."

12. Project Management Institute, "The Disciplined Agile Foundation Layer."

13. Project Management Institute, *PMBOK Guide*, 558.

A free ebook edition is available with the purchase of this book.

To claim your free ebook edition:
1. Visit MorganJamesBOGO.com
2. Sign your name CLEARLY in the space
3. Complete the form and submit a photo of the entire copyright page
4. You or your friend can download the ebook to your preferred device

Morgan James BOGO™

A **FREE** ebook edition is available for you or a friend with the purchase of this print book.

CLEARLY SIGN YOUR NAME ABOVE

Instructions to claim your free ebook edition:
1. Visit MorganJamesBOGO.com
2. Sign your name CLEARLY in the space above
3. Complete the form and submit a photo of this entire page
4. You or your friend can download the ebook to your preferred device

Print & Digital Together Forever.

 Snap a photo

 Free ebook

 Read anywhere

CPSIA information can be obtained
at www.ICGtesting.com
Printed in the USA
LVHW090234050222
710188LV00001B/55